The
Princeton
Review

# Crash Course for the
# GRE

### 3rd Edition

Wendy Voelkle

PrincetonReview.com

Random House, Inc. New York

Princeton Review Publishing, Inc.
2315 Broadway
New York, NY 10024

E-mail: editorialsupport@review.com

Copyright © 2007 by Princeton Review Publishing, Inc.

Published in the United States by Random House, Inc., New York, and
simultaneously in Canada by Random House of Canada Limited, Toronto.

ISBN 978-0-375-76572-8
ISSN 1545-620x
Editor: Rebecca Lessem
Designer: Stephanie Martin
Production Editor: Katie O'Neill
Production Coordinator: Suzanne Barker

Printed in the United States of America.

10   9   8   7   6   5   4   3   2   1

Third Edition

# ACKNOWLEDGMENTS

The author would like to thank the following people for their help: Marina Padakis, Laurie Barnett, John Bergdahl, Jackie Jendras, Julieanna Lambert, Stephanie Martin, Neil McMahon, Melody Marcus, Briana Gordon, Rebecca Lessem, Katie O'Neill, M. Tighe Wall, Stephen White, Suzanne Barker, Kim Howie, and Jeff Rubenstein.

Special thanks to Adam Robinson, who conceived of and perfected the Joe Bloggs approach to standardized tests and many of the other successful techniques used by The Princteon Review.

# ABOUT THE AUTHOR

Karen Lurie is the author of five books, including *Cracking the GRE* and the *LSAT/GRE Analytic Workout*. She lives in New York City.

# CONTENTS

# PART I

# INTRODUCTION

# ORIENTATION

## WHAT IS *CRASH COURSE FOR THE GRE?*

*Crash Course for the GRE* is just what it sounds like—a quick but thorough guide to the basic material on the GRE computer-adaptive test (also called the GRE CAT, or GRE computer-based test). It includes helpful techniques for nailing as many questions as possible, even if you don't have a lot of time to prepare. *Crash Course for the GRE* is *not* a comprehensive study guide for the GRE. If you're looking for that, you should try The Princeton Review's *Cracking the GRE CAT.*

## WHAT IS THE GRE?

The Graduate Record Examination (GRE) is a multiple-choice aptitude test intended for applicants to graduate schools. It definitely does *not* measure your intelligence, nor does it measure how well you will do in graduate school. The GRE is a test of how well you handle standardized tests. Luckily, this is a skill you can improve with practice.

The three sections of the GRE that count toward your score are (not necessarily in this order):

- one 30-minute, 30-question Verbal Reasoning section

- one 45-minute, 28-question Quantitative Reasoning (Math) section

- one 75-minute, 25-question Analytical Writing section

The Verbal section of the GRE CAT contains four types of questions (in no particular order):

- 8 to 10 antonyms

- 5 to 7 sentence completions

- 6 to 8 analogies

- 2 to 4 reading comprehension passages with a total of 6 to 10 questions

The Math section contains two types of questions (in no particular order):

- 13 to 15 quantitative comparisons (with four answer choices)

- 12 to 16 problem-solving questions, including 4 to 6 chart questions from 2 to 3 charts (with five answer choices)

The Analytical Writing section contains two types of questions (in no particular order):

- Analyze an Issue

- Analyze an Argument

## Sections That Don't Count

You'll probably have a fourth, unidentified experimental section: another Verbal or Math section. It can be anywhere on the test. This section will not count toward your score. You can't avoid it, and you won't even recognize it. If you get two Verbal sections, then one of them is experimental, but you won't know which one. So, don't worry about it. Just do your best on all questions, and plan to be at the test center for about four hours.

Occasionally there will also be an optional, identified, unscored research section (sometimes called a "pretest"), consisting of additional experimental questions. It will probably be a writing measure or some different math questions. If your test includes this section, it will be last. Fortunately, because you will have completed all scored sections of the test at this point, The Educational Testing Service's (ETS) use of you as a guinea pig can have no adverse effect on your GRE score. Data obtained from this research section will be used to revise the test over the next few years.

## What Does a GRE Score Look Like?

You will receive separate Verbal and Quantitative scores, each on a scale that runs from 200 to 800 in ten point increments. Your Analytical Writing score is on a scale of 0 to 6 in half-point increments.

## Where Does the GRE Come From?

Like most standardized tests in this country, the GRE is published by ETS, a big, tax-exempt private company in New Jersey. ETS publishes the GRE under the sponsorship of the Graduate Record Examinations Board, an organization affiliated with the Association of Graduate Schools and the Council of Graduate Schools in the United States.

The GRE isn't written by distinguished professors, renowned scholars, or graduate-school admissions officers. For the most part, it's written by ordinary ETS employees, sometimes with freelance help from local graduate students. There's no reason to be intimidated by these people.

## Why Should I Listen to The Princeton Review?

We monitor the GRE. Our teaching methods for cracking it were developed through exhaustive analysis of all available GREs and careful research into the methods by which standardized tests are constructed. Our focus is on the basic concepts that will enable you to attack any problem, strip it down to its essential components, and solve it in as little time as possible.

## GRE CAT FACTS

You can take the GRE CAT on almost any day from October through January, and almost any day during the first three weeks of the months of February through June. You may take the test only once per calendar month. Appointments are scheduled on a first-come, first-served basis. There's no real deadline for registering for the test (technically, you can register the day before), but there's a limited number of seats available on any given day, and centers do fill up, sometimes weeks in advance. It's good to give yourself at least a couple of weeks of lead time to register.

You can schedule a test session for the GRE CAT (which, by the way, will cost you $130) by calling The Sylvan Technologies National Registration Center at (800) GRE-CALL. Or, you can register online at **www.gre.org**. General inquiries about the GRE can be made by calling Educational Testing Services at (609) 771-7670. You may also call your local test center to set up an appointment (a list of centers is available from ETS; most are Sylvan Learning Centers). In order to schedule your test by phone, you must pay by VISA or Mastercard. Check your GRE Registration Booklet or **www.gre.org** for more information because test prices may change.

You will receive your Verbal and Math scores right after you finish the exam. You will have to wait about two weeks to get your Analytical Writing Score.

The lack of a physical test booklet makes it impossible to write directly on the problems themselves (to cross out incorrect answers, etc.), but you'll get scratch paper, so your work space is limitless. Using scratch paper is one of the keys to scoring well on the GRE CAT.

## WHAT THE GRE CAT LOOKS LIKE

When there's a question on the screen, it will look like the following:

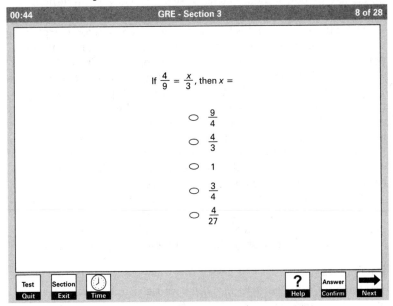

If $\frac{4}{9} = \frac{x}{3}$, then $x =$

○ $\frac{9}{4}$

○ $\frac{4}{3}$

○ 1

○ $\frac{3}{4}$

○ $\frac{4}{27}$

| Test Quit | Section Exit | Time | | ? Help | Answer Confirm | Next |

The problem you're working on will be in the middle of the screen. The answer choices will have little bubbles next to them. To choose an answer, click on the bubble that corresponds with the choice you are picking.

A readout of the time remaining in the section may be displayed if you choose; the number of questions you've done and the total number of questions in the section will be displayed in the upper right corner. The bottom of the screen will contain the following buttons, from left to right:

**Test Quit:** You can end the test at any time by clicking on this button. However, unless you become violently ill, we do not recommend that you ever do this. Even if you decide not to have this test scored (an option you get when you're done with the exam), you should finish the test. After all, it's great practice for when you finally want the test to count. Besides, you can't get a refund from ETS.

**Section Exit:** You'll be taken out of the section you're working on by clicking on this button, and *you won't get a score.* If you happen to finish a section before the time is up, just sit and rest till the next section begins.

**Time:** You may opt to display or hide the digital countdown by clicking on this button. Some people like to have it on the screen; others like to look at their watches instead. Whatever you decide, when time is almost up, the display will appear on the screen.

**Help:** If you click on this button, you'll get a little tutorial explaining what the different buttons mean and how to use them. Unfortunately, you won't get any help with the actual material on the screen!

**Answer Confirm:** ETS makes you confirm your choice to make sure you're certain you want to go on to the next question. When you click on "Next," the "Answer Confirm" icon lights up. If you're sticking with your answer, click on "Answer Confirm," and the computer records this answer and gives you the next question.

**Next:** After you've answered the question you're working on by clicking the bubble next to the answer choice you think is correct, click on this button to go on to the next screen.

As you prepare for the GRE, work through every question as if it is being presented on a computer screen. That means using scrap paper, copying things down on it, and not doing *anything* in your head. You'll learn more about how to do that throughout this book.

## Real Tests

You bought *Crash Course for the GRE* because you don't have a lot of time to prepare, and you want the basics. But you still need real GRE questions on which to practice. The only source of real GREs is the publisher of the test, ETS. Therefore, if you have the time, we recommend that you download GRE POWERPREP® Software—Test Preparation for the General Test, which includes GRE questions presented in the CAT mode from **www.gre.org**. You will also receive a copy on CD-ROM when you register for the GRE.

## Stay Current

The information in this book is accurate right now, and will be updated yearly. However, the publishing business is such that if the test changed tomorrow, the book might be a little behind. For the most current information possible, visit ETS's website at **www.gre.org**, or our website at **PrincetonReview.com**.

# GENERAL STRATEGY

# HOW A COMPUTER-ADAPTIVE TEST WORKS

Computer-adaptive tests (CAT) use your performance on one question to determine which question you will be asked next. ETS assumes that you have the average score in a particular category—for example, a 480 in Verbal. You'll be asked a question of difficulty appropriate to this score level. If you answer correctly, the computer adjusts your score to a new level, say 550, and your next question is more difficult. If you answer incorrectly, your score will drop and your next question will be less difficult. The amount your score will change with each new correct or incorrect answer is reduced as you move farther into the test, so by the end of the exam, the computer will have effectively zeroed in on your GRE score. That's the theory, anyway.

So, when you get an answer right, your next question is harder; when you get an answer wrong, your next question is easier. You won't know how you did on the prior question, so just focus on doing your best on each question. *Never, ever try to figure out how difficult a question is supposed to be.*

## WHAT DOES ALL THIS MEAN?

It means that how much credit you get for a question depends on how you've done on the previous questions. If you've correctly answered all the questions before it, you're going to get more credit for answering a question correctly than you would if you had missed a bunch of questions before you worked your way to that question. In a nutshell: Your responses to the first questions in a section will have a greater impact on your final score than your responses to those later in the section, after the computer has already determined your score range. Your score moves up and down in larger increments at the beginning of the test than it does toward the end. *The first third to half of each section determines the bulk of your score. So be extra careful on the first third to half of each section.*

### Answer Every Question

You will be penalized for not giving an answer to every question in a section. Basically, your raw score will be reduced by the percentage of unanswered questions in a section (e.g., a thirty-question section with six questions left blank will mean a 20 percent reduction of your raw score). *So, do not leave any question unanswered.*

## Let the Computer Help You

During the last two or three minutes of a section, the time display on the computer screen will start flashing, showing you the remaining time in both minutes and seconds. Let this be your signal to start wrapping things up by guessing your favorite letter for whatever questions you have left in the section. You don't want to leave any questions unanswered in any section.

## HOW TO GUESS

Because the computer "decides" what to do next based on how you answer the question on the screen, you *must* answer that question. There is no skipping a question and coming back to it later, and no changing an answer later.

Once you've worked carefully through the first third to half of the section, you don't want to get bogged down with time-consuming questions. If you encounter a question that seems extremely difficult or time-consuming, eliminate answers that you know are wrong, and make an educated guess (you're about to learn how). This will allow you to get to subsequent questions, which may be easier, with enough time to work them.

You're probably going to see questions on which you'll have to guess. But we're not talking about random guessing. After all, the right answer is on the screen. ETS doesn't care how you get your answer; it only cares about whether you clicked on the credited response with your mouse. You might as well benefit from this by getting questions right even when you really don't know the answer. And you can do that with the Process of Elimination, or POE. POE is your new religion. Learn it. Live it. Love it.

## The Amazing Power of POE

There are roughly four times as many wrong answers as there are right answers; it's often easier to identify the wrong answers than to identify the best one. By using POE, you'll be able to improve your score on the GRE by looking for wrong answers instead of right ones on questions you're having trouble with.

Why? Because every time you're able to eliminate an incorrect choice on a GRE question, you improve your odds of finding the best answer. The more incorrect choices you eliminate, the better your odds. Don't be afraid to arrive at ETS's answer *indirectly*. You'll be avoiding the traps laid in your path by the test writers, traps that are designed to catch unwary test takers who try to approach the problems *directly*.

If you guessed blindly on a five-choice GRE problem, you would have one chance in five of picking ETS's answer. Eliminate one incorrect choice, and your chances improve to one in four. Eliminate three, and you have a fifty-fifty chance of earning points by guessing. Get the picture? You must answer each question to get to the next one, so you'll have to guess sometimes. Why not improve your odds?

> **Note:** Especially on verbal questions, if you're not sure what a word in an answer choice means, don't eliminate that choice. It might be the answer! Only eliminate answers you know are wrong.

## The "Best" Answer

The instructions on the GRE tell you to select the "best" answer to each question. ETS calls them "best" answers, or the "credited responses," instead of "correct" answers, to protect itself from the complaints of test takers who might be tempted to quarrel with ETS's judgment. You have to pick from the choices ETS gives you, and sometimes you might not like any of them. Your job is to find the one answer for which ETS gives credit.

## Use That Paper!

For POE to work, it's crucial that you keep track of what choices you're eliminating. By crossing out a clearly incorrect choice, you permanently eliminate it from consideration. If you don't cross it out, you'll keep considering it. Crossing out incorrect choices can make it much easier to find the credited response, because there will be fewer places where it can hide. But how can you cross anything out on a computer screen?

**By using your scratch paper!** On the GRE, the answer choices have empty bubbles next to them, but in this book, we'll refer to them as (A), (B), (C), (D), and (E). Each time you see a question, get in the habit of immediately writing down A, B, C, D, E on your scratch paper.

| A | A | A | A |
|---|---|---|---|
| B | B | B | B |
| C | C | C | C |
| D | D | D | D |
| E | E | E | E |

| A | A | A | A |
|---|---|---|---|
| B | B | B | B |
| C | C | C | C |
| D | D | D | D |
| E | E | E | E |

Mark up at least a couple of pages (front and back) like this before the test officially starts. This will give you a bunch of distinct work areas per page, which will be especially helpful for the Math section. You don't want to get confused when your work from one question runs into your work from a previous question.

You then can physically cross off choices that you're eliminating. **Do it every time you do a GRE question,** whether in this book or elsewhere. Get used to writing on scratch paper instead of near the question, because you won't be able to write near the question on test day.

## Don't Do Anything in Your Head

Besides eliminating incorrect answers, there are many other ways to use scratch paper to solve questions; you're going to learn them all. Just remember: Even if you're tempted to try to solve questions in your head, even if you think that writing things down on your scratch paper is a waste of time, you're wrong. Trust us. **Always write everything down.**

## Read and Copy Carefully

You can do all the calculations right and still get a question wrong. How? What if you solve for $x$ but the question was "What is the value of $x + 3$?" Ugh. Always *reread* the question. Take your time and don't be careless. The question will stay on the screen; it's not going anywhere.

Or, how about this? The radius of the circle is 6, but when you copied the picture onto your scratch paper, you accidentally made it 5. Ugh! Many of the mistakes you make at first might stem from copying information down incorrectly. Learn from your mistakes! You need to be extra careful when copying down information.

## Accuracy vs. Speed

You don't get points for speed; the only thing that matters is accuracy. Take some time to work through each problem carefully (as long as you leave some time at the end of the section to fill out the rest of it). If you're making careless errors, you won't even realize you're missing questions. Get into the habit of double-checking all of your answers before you choose them. However, don't get too bogged down on a question. If you're totally stuck, guess and move on.

## At the Testing Center

You'll be asked for two forms of identification; one must be a photo ID. Then, an employee will take a digital photograph of you before taking you to the computer station where you will take the test. You get a desk, a computer, a keyboard, a mouse, about six pieces of scratch paper, and a pencil. Before the test begins, make sure your desk is sturdy and you have enough light, and don't be afraid to speak up if you want to move.

If there are other people in the room, they might not be taking the GRE CAT. They could be taking a nursing test, or a licensing exam for architects. And they will not necessarily have started their exams at the same time. The testing center employee will get you set up at your computer, but from then on, the computer itself will act as your proctor. It'll tell you how much time you have left in a section, when time is up, and when to move on to the next section.

The test center employees will be available because they will be monitoring the testing room for security purposes with closed-circuit television. But don't worry, you won't even notice. If you have a question, or need to request more scratch paper during the test, try to do so between the timed sections.

## Let It Go

When you begin a new section, focus on that section and put the last one behind you. Don't think about that pesky antonym from an earlier section while a geometry question is on your screen. You can't go back, and besides, your impression of how you did on a section is probably much worse than reality. Remember, the test adapts so that it is hard for everyone.

## This Is the End

When you're done with the test, the computer will ask you twice if you want this test to count. If you say "no," the computer will not record your score, no schools will ever see it, and neither will you. You can't look at your score and then decide whether you want to keep it or not. And you can't change your mind later. If you say you want the test to count, the computer will give you your Verbal and Math scores right there on the screen. A few weeks later, you'll receive your verified score in the mail. You can't change your mind and cancel it.

## TEST DAY CHECKLIST

Dress in layers so that you'll be comfortable regardless of whether the room is cool or warm.

Don't bother bringing a calculator; you're not allowed to use one.

Be sure to have breakfast, or lunch, depending on the time your test is scheduled (but don't eat anything, you know, "weird"). And go easy on the liquids and caffeine.

Do a few GRE practice problems to warm up your brain. Don't try to tackle difficult new questions, but review a few questions that you've done before to help you review the problem-solving strategies for each section of the GRE CAT. This will also help you put your "game-face" on and get you into test mode.

Make sure to bring two forms of identification (one with a recent photograph) to the test center. Acceptable forms of identification include driver's licenses, photo-bearing employee ID cards, and valid passports.

If you registered by mail, you must also bring the authorization voucher sent to you by ETS.

## The Week of the Test

A week before the test is not the time for any major life changes. This is *not* the week to quit smoking, start smoking, quit drinking coffee, start drinking coffee, start a relationship, end a relationship, or quit a job. Business as usual, okay?

# PART II

# TEN STEPS
## TO THE GRE

# STEP 1
# MAKE A SENTENCE:
# ANALOGIES

## WHAT IS AN ANALOGY?

On an analogy, your job is to figure out the relationship between the original pair of words (we'll call them the *stem words*) and find an answer choice in which the words have the same relationship. Let's look at one:

EVICT : TENANT ::

○ patronize : child
○ sanction : nation
○ enclose : wall
○ disbar : lawyer
○ ostracize : pariah

The stem words are EVICT and TENANT. What's the relationship?

## THE BIG TECHNIQUE: MAKE A SENTENCE

If you can define both of the stem words, your first step is to make a simple sentence that shows their relationship. Think about defining one in terms of the other, and don't get fancy or tell a story. If you looked up EVICT in the dictionary, and the definition had TENANT in it, what might it say? Something like this: EVICT means to throw out a TENANT. That's your sentence.

### The Usual Sentences

A few relationships appear over and over on the GRE. Learn them!

| | |
|---|---|
| **Degree:** | ADMIRE : IDOLIZE—IDOLIZE means to ADMIRE a lot. |
| **Type of:** | FRUIT : ORANGE—an ORANGE is a type of FRUIT. |
| **Part of:** | CHAPTER : BOOK—a CHAPTER is a part of a BOOK. |
| **Function of:** | BRAIN : COGNITION—the function of a BRAIN is COGNITION. |
| **Characterized by:** | ZEALOT : FERVOR—a ZEALOT is characterized by FERVOR. |
| **With/without:** | POOR : MONEY—POOR means without MONEY. |

## Your Turn

### Drill 1

Practice making sentences from the following stem word pairs, defining one word in terms of the other (answers can be found at the end of the chapter):

1. GIGANTIC : LARGE _____
2. FADE : BRILLIANCE _____
3. DICTIONARY : WORDS _____
4. ADHESIVE : BIND _____
5. LETTERS : ALPHABET _____
6. ETERNAL : END _____
7. COTTAGE : HOUSE _____
8. VERSE : POEM _____
9. SYLLABUS : COURSE _____
10. ANTISEPTIC : SANITIZE _____

## Write It Down!

If you try to make your sentence in your head, you might forget it after you try a few answer choices or, even worse, change it to agree with one of the answer choices. That defeats the whole purpose!

Always write your sentence on your scratch paper. If you make your sentence from right to left (yes, that's allowed), draw an arrow for that question to remind you to plug in the answer choices from right to left. Then write A, B, C, D, E to represent the five answer choices.

## POE

The words in the credited response have to fit exactly into the sentence you made for the original pair of words. If you know the words in the answer choice, and they don't fit into the sentence, eliminate that choice by crossing it off on your scratch paper. If you're not sure you can define the words in an answer choice, don't eliminate that choice.

Here's the example again:

EVICT : TENANT ::
- patronize : child
- sanction : nation
- enclose : wall
- disbar : lawyer
- ostracize : pariah

Our sentence was "EVICT means to throw out a TENANT." Let's go to the answer choices:

(A) Is patronize to throw out a child? Nope.

(B) Is sanction to throw out a nation? Nope.

(C) Is enclose to throw out a wall? Nope.

(D) Is disbar to throw out a lawyer? Yes.

(E) Is ostracize to throw out a pariah? Nope, a pariah has already been thrown out.

The best answer is (D).

**What If I Don't Know Some of the Words in the Answer Choices?**
Let's say you'd never seen one of the words in answer choice (E) before. How would you know whether they worked in your sentence?

Assuming you know both stem words, you can still ask yourself whether any word could create a relationship in the choice identical to the relationship in the stem. If not, you can eliminate the choice. Then, see what you have left and take an educated guess.

## MAKE A SENTENCE, PART 2: WORKING BACKWARD

It's all very nice when you know the stem words. But if you don't know the stem words, you can't make a sentence. So, what should you do?

Because the words in the correct answer choice must have a relationship similar to that of the stem words, they must also have a relationship to each other. So if the words in an answer choice *do not* have a good relationship, that choice cannot be correct.

For example, if you saw "car : seat" in the answer choices, you could get rid of that choice. Why? Because car and seat are not necessarily related. Yes, cars usually have seats, but try making one of those "defining" sentences with car and seat. You can't do it, right?

If you looked up "seat" in the dictionary, would "car" be there? Nope.
If you looked up "car" in the dictionary, would "seat" be there? Nope.

## Your Turn

## Drill 2

Decide which of the following pairs have a clear relationship by making sentences with them. If you think a pair of words has no relationship, put an "X" next to that pair. If you don't know the words well enough to tell whether they are related, leave the question blank (answers can be found at the end of the chapter):

1. needle : thread _____

2. vernal : spring _____

3. breach : dam _____

4. dog : cat _____

5. vacillate : steadfast _____

6. scintilla : minuscule _____

7. calumniate : reputation _____

8. sedulous : piquancy _____

9. witty : mordant _____

10. mendacity : truth _____

## When You Can't Make a Sentence

So, if you can't make a sentence with the stem words, start by going to the answers and eliminating choices that aren't really related. But what do you do with the answers that are left?

Let's look at an example that's missing a stem word (just pretend it's a word you don't know):

??? : CORN ::

○ flower : stem
○ cube : water
○ cow : milk
○ loaf : pan
○ pod : pea

Because we can't make a sentence with the stem words, we have to go to the answers.

(A) Are flower and stem related? Try making a sentence. We could say "The stem is the base of a flower." Now we take that sentence and work backward with the stem word we know: Can CORN be the base of something? No. That means we can eliminate (A).

(B) Are cube and water related? Try making a sentence. No. Eliminate (B).

(C) Are cow and milk related? Try making a sentence. We could say, "Milk comes from a cow." Does CORN come from something? Not in the same way. Eliminate (C).

(D) Are loaf and pan related? Try making a sentence. Nope. Eliminate (D).

(E) Are pod and pea related? Try making a sentence. We could say, "A pea is found in a pod" or "A pod holds peas." Is CORN found in something? Does something hold corn? Yes, an EAR. Even if you don't think of the word EAR, you can still imagine that something that holds corn exists. So (E) is the best answer (the missing word was, in fact, EAR).

So, you're always making sentences when you do analogies, whether you know the stem words or not.

Let's put it all together:

> INVARIABLE : CHANGE ::
> ○ incurable : disease
> ○ unfathomable : depth
> ○ extraneous : proposition
> ○ ineffable : expression
> ○ variegated : appearance

Your sentence for the relationship between the stem words would be something like "Something INVARIABLE is without CHANGE." Notice that CHANGE is a noun, not a verb. How did we know? We checked the corresponding words in the answer choices. Because disease, depth, proposition, expression, and appearance are nouns, CHANGE must be a noun, too.

(A) Is something incurable without disease? No. Eliminate this choice.

(B) Is something unfathomable without depth? Nope. Eliminate this choice, too.

(C) Is something extraneous without proposition? Do you know the dictionary definition of "extraneous"? Keep this choice and check out the other choices.

(D) Is something ineffable without expression? If you don't know the definition of "ineffable," you'd better keep this choice.

(E) Is something variegated without appearance? Now, you may not know the exact definition of "variegated," but from what we sort of know, it wouldn't fit our sentence. It has something to do with appearance, but it doesn't mean without appearance.

Now we're guessing between choices (C) and (D). Do you think it's more likely that some word means "without proposition" or that some word means "without expression"? (D) is the answer.

Here's another one:

BELIEF : RECANTATION ::
- ◯ statement : retraction
- ◯ opinion : justification
- ◯ doctrine : devotion
- ◯ legislation : amendment
- ◯ pronouncement : oration

Let's say you're not sure what RECANTATION means. Time to go to the answers.

(A) Are statement and retraction related? Try making a sentence. "Retraction is to take back a statement." Could RECANTATION mean to take back a BELIEF? Maybe, so leave in (A).

(B) Are opinion and justification related? Try making a sentence. Nope. Eliminate (B).

(C) Are doctrine and devotion related? No, but if you weren't sure of the words, you'd have to leave it in.

(D) Are legislation and amendment related? It sounds good, but try making a sentence. Does legislation always have to do with amendments? Nope. Eliminate (D).

(E) Are pronouncement and oration related? No, but if you weren't sure of the words, you'd have to leave it in. The best answer is (A), although some of you might have been guessing (C) or (E), depending on your vocabulary level. It's still better than a blind guess.

## The Last Resort

If you've eliminated all the answer choices with words that you know or sort of know, and you're left with a couple of choices containing words that you've never seen before, just guess and move on. Your GRE score is going to be much higher if you are guessing between two choices than it would be if you hadn't eliminated those other three choices by using our techniques.

# ANSWERS

## Drill 1

1. GIGANTIC means very LARGE.

2. FADE means to lose BRILLIANCE.

3. A DICTIONARY contains WORDS.

4  An ADHESIVE is used to BIND.

5. LETTERS make up the ALPHABET.

6. ETERNAL means without END.

7. A COTTAGE is a type of HOUSE.

8. A VERSE is a part of a POEM.

9. A SYLLABUS is a plan for a COURSE.

10. An ANTISEPTIC is used to SANITIZE.

## Drill 2

1. A needle pulls thread.

2. Vernal means related to spring.

3. A breach is a rift in a dam.

4. Unrelated. Dogs and cats are both pets, but there is no relationship between them.

5. To be steadfast is not to vacillate.

6. A scintilla is a minuscule amount.

7. To calumniate is to ruin the reputation of.

8. Unrelated.

9. To be mordant is to be bitingly witty.

10. Mendacity is not telling the truth.

# STEP 2

# SPEAK FOR YOURSELF: SENTENCE COMPLETIONS

## "I ALREADY KNOW HOW TO DO THESE"

Sentence completions—which you've known since kindergarten as fill-in-the-blanks—look very familiar. But beware! The way ETS designs these problems is very different from the way your elementary school teachers did. Here's what a sentence completion looks like:

> Wilson worked _____ on his first novel, cloistering himself in his study for days on end without food or sleep.
>
> ○ carelessly
> ○ creatively
> ○ tirelessly
> ○ intermittently
> ○ voluntarily

Many testers read sentence completions quickly, then go immediately to the choices and begin plugging them into the blanks. This is exactly what ETS wants you to do, so the answer choices will distract you from the meaning of the sentence. This approach may work occasionally on easy problems, but it definitely won't work on more difficult ones. Why take the chance?

## THE BIG TECHNIQUE: SPEAK FOR YOURSELF

Physically cover the answer choices on the screen, read the sentence, and write down your own words for the blank(s) before you look at the answer choices. This way, you won't let the answer choices distract you and thereby play into ETS's hands.

Let's try that sentence completion *without* answer choices:

> Wilson worked _____ on his first novel, cloistering himself in his study for days on end without food or sleep.

Your job is to speak for yourself by filling in the blank with your own word. It doesn't have to be a fancy vocabulary word. It just has to make sense to you in the blank. In this case, the blank is describing the way Wilson worked. Let's use everything we know about the way he worked to help us. We know he's not eating or sleeping, and he's been in his study for days on end (don't worry if you don't know what "cloistering" means). We need a word in the blank that describes working for days on end without food or sleep. How about "hard"? See, it's nothing fancy, but it'll work. So, write down "hard" on your scrap paper (and A, B, C, D, E for eliminating choices, of course).

Now let's bring in the answer choices that went with this question:

- ○ carelessly
- ○ creatively
- ○ tirelessly
- ○ intermittently
- ○ voluntarily

All we have to do is go through them, eliminating anything that doesn't mean "hard."

(A) Does "carelessly" mean hard? No. Eliminate.

(B) Does "creatively" mean hard? No. Get rid of this choice.

(C) Does "tirelessly" mean hard? Maybe, because we know that Wilson worked "for days on end without food or sleep." Keep this choice.

(D) Does "intermittently" mean hard? Be careful! Are you sure you know the dictionary definition of the word? If not, keep this choice and continue.

(E) Does "voluntarily" mean hard? Definitely not. Eliminate.

We're down to two possible choices, but we know that "tirelessly" fits, because we know that Wilson worked "for days on end without food or sleep." So the best answer is (C).

## Look Before You Leap: The Clue

The clue is the part of the sentence that describes the blank. It's the most descriptive part of the sentence. There was a clue in that sentence that told us how Wilson worked. It was the phrase "days on end." Without it, any number of different words could plausibly fill in the blank. Finding the clue helped us anticipate ETS's answer. Every GRE sentence completion has at least one clue in it. Count on it.

## Your Turn

### Drill 1

In each of the following sentences, find the clue and underline it. Then, write down your own word for the blank. It doesn't matter if your guesses are awkward or wordy. All you need to do is express the right idea.

1. Despite the apparent _____ of the demands, the negotiations dragged on for over a year.

2. Most students found Dr. Schwartz's lecture on art excessively detailed and academic; some thought his display of _____ exasperating.

### Drill 2

Now look at the same questions again, this time with the answer choices provided. Use your words above to eliminate answer choices (answers can be found at the end of the chapter):

1. Despite the apparent _____ of the demands, the negotiations dragged on for over a year.
   (A) hastiness
   (B) intolerance
   (C) publicity
   (D) modesty
   (E) desirability

2. Most students found Dr. Schwartz's lecture on art excessively detailed and academic; some thought his display of _____ exasperating.
   (A) pedantry
   (B) logic
   (C) aesthetics
   (D) erudition
   (E) literalism

## Look Before You Leap—Trigger Words and Punctuation

Certain words signal changes in the meaning of a sentence. We call them "trigger words." They provide important structural indicators of the meaning of the sentence, and are often the key to figuring out what words have to mean to fill in the blanks in a sentence completion. Here are some of the most important sentence completion trigger words and punctuation:

| | |
|---|---|
| but | in contrast |
| although (though, even though) | unfortunately |
| unless | heretofore |
| rather | thus |
| yet | and |
| despite | therefore |
| while | similarly |
| however | ; *or* : |

Paying attention to trigger words is crucial to understanding the meaning of the sentence, thereby helping you to speak for yourself. The words from *but* to *heretofore* are "change direction" trigger words, indicating that the two parts of the sentence diverge in meaning. The above words, from *thus* to the colon (:) and semi-colon (;), are "some direction" triggers, indicating that the two parts of the above sentence agree. For example, if your sentence said "Judy was a fair and _____ judge," the placement of the "and" would tell you that the word in the blank would have to be similar to "fair." You could even use the word "fair" as your fill-in-the-blank word.

What if your sentence said, "Judy was a fair but _____ judge"? The placement of the "but" would tell you that the word in the blank would have to be somewhat opposite of "fair," something like "tough."

Let's try this one (we're taking the answer choices away again, for now):

> Although originally created for
> _____ use, the colorful, stamped tin
> kitchen boxes of the early twentieth
> century are now prized primarily for
> their ornamental qualities.

What's the clue in the sentence that tells us why the boxes were originally created? Well, we know that they "are now prized primarily for their ornamental qualities." Does this mean that they were originally created for "ornamental" use? No. The trigger word "although" indicates that the word for the blank will mean the opposite of "ornamental." How about "useful"? It may sound strange to say "useful use," but don't worry about how your words sound—it's what they mean that's important.

Now, here are the answer choices:

- ○ traditional
- ○ practical
- ○ occasional
- ○ annual
- ○ commercial

(A) Does "traditional" mean useful? No. Eliminate.

(B) Does "practical" mean useful? Yes. But let's just check the remaining choices.

(C) Does "occasional" mean useful? No. Get rid of it.

(D) Does "annual" mean useful? Nope.

(E) Does "commercial" mean useful? No. Eliminate it. The best answer is (B).

## Positive/Negative

In some cases, you may think of several words that could go in the blanks. Or, you might not be able to think of any. Rather than spend a lot of time trying to find the "perfect" word, just ask yourself whether the missing word will be a positive word or a negative word. Then, write a + or a – symbol on your scratch paper and take it from there. Here's an example (again, without answer choices, for now):

Trembling with anger, the belligerent colonel ordered his men to _____ the civilians.

Use those clues. We know the colonel is "trembling with anger," and that he's "belligerent" (which means war-like). Is the missing word a "good" word or a "bad" word? It's a "bad" word. The colonel is clearly going to do something nasty to the civilians. Now we can go to the answer choices and eliminate any choices that are positive and therefore couldn't be correct:

- ○ congratulate
- ○ promote
- ○ reward
- ○ attack
- ○ worship

Choices A, B, C, and E are all positive words; therefore, they can all be eliminated. The only negative word among the choices is (D), the best answer. Positive/negative won't work for every question, but sometimes it can get you out of a jam.

## TWO BLANKS

Many sentence completions will have two blanks rather than just one. The key to getting them right is concentrating on one of the blanks at a time. A two-blank answer choice can be the best answer choice only if it works for both of the blanks. If you can determine that one of the words in the choice doesn't work in its corresponding blank, you can eliminate that choice without checking the other word.

Which blank should you concentrate on? The one for which you have a better clue. Once you've decided which blank you have a better clue for, and have written down a word for it, go to the answer choices and look only at the ones provided for that blank. Then eliminate any choice that doesn't work for that blank.

Let's try one:

A growing number of heretical scientists are claiming the once _____ theory of evolution must be _____, if not actually shelved.

After reading the whole sentence, it seems that the second blank is easier to start with, because you've got the clue "if not actually shelved" to help you. It tells you that the second blank must mean something like "almost shelved" or "changed in some basically negative way." Now look at the choices, paying attention only to the second word in each (the first words have been deleted to help you ignore them):

○ _____ . . postulated
○ _____ . . popularized
○ _____ . . reexamined
○ _____ . . modified
○ _____ . . promulgated

Eliminate anything that doesn't mean "almost shelved." Choice (B) can definitely go. If you don't know what the words in (A) and (E) mean, you must leave them in. But as far as words we know that would fit with "almost shelved," how about choices (C) and (D)? To "reexamine" or "modify" a theory is to alter it in some way that falls short of actually throwing it out.

Now let's go back to the first blank. If this theory is almost going to be shelved, it's not universally accepted anymore. And, the scientists who want it shelved are heretical, which means they are going against accepted beliefs. The word "once" is in front of the first blank, and we now know that the theory was once universally accepted, because now it isn't. So, let's put "universally accepted" in the first blank. Now look at the first word in the choices we liked, (C) and (D):

○ sacrosanct . . reexamined
○ modern . . modified

There's no reason to believe it's "modern," and "sacrosanct" means "inviolably sacred," or universally accepted. So, the best answer is (C). If we didn't like either of those, we'd check the words that went with (A) and (E), the words we didn't know.

## Positive/Negative

Trigger words and punctuation are also especially important on sentence completions with two blanks, which means there will be times you need to use the positive/negative technique to help you speak for yourself.

Trigger words like "although" and "but" show that the relationship between the two blanks involves an opposition (–/+ or +/–). Trigger words like "and" show that the relationship between the two blanks involves a similarity (–/– or +/+). Crossing out choices that don't fit the pattern will help you zero in on the answer.

> Although he was usually _____ and _____, his illness blunted both his appetite and his temper.

The trigger word "although" tells us that if his illness blunted both his appetite and his temper now, they both (because of the trigger word "and") must normally be unblunted or extreme. So, both of the words in the blanks will be negative words. Now we can eliminate any choice that has a positive word anywhere in it:

- ○ gluttonous . . contentious
- ○ sated . . belligerent
- ○ avaricious . . responsive
- ○ eloquent . . reflective
- ○ ravenous . . reticent

Immediately eliminate choices (C) and (D) because of "responsive" and "eloquent." If you "sort of" know that "sated" is a positive word, eliminate choice (B) also. "Ravenous" would work in the first blank, but "reticent," or quiet, isn't necessarily negative. The best answer is (A). Look up the vocabulary words that you didn't know!

# ANSWERS

## Drill 2

1. D
2. A

# STEP 3
# KNOW THYSELF: ANTONYMS

## YES, THERE REALLY ARE TECHNIQUES

You may think that doing well on antonyms, where your sole task is to pick the word opposite in meaning to the stem word, all comes down to vocabulary—that is, if you have a big vocabulary, you'll do well on antonyms, and if you have a tiny vocabulary, you'll have trouble. And yes, the best way to improve your antonym score is to improve your vocabulary, but you don't have much time. Don't worry—we have techniques that can enable you to squeeze the maximum number of points out of any vocabulary.

## THE BIG TECHNIQUE: KNOW THYSELF

From now on, think of vocabulary words in terms of these three categories:

Words you know: These are words you can define accurately. If you can't give a definition of a word that's pretty close to what a dictionary would say, then it's not a word you know.

Words you "sort of" know: These are words you've seen or heard before, or maybe even used yourself, but can't define accurately. You may have a sense of how these words are used, but beware! You have to treat these words very differently from the words you can define. After you encounter a word you sort of know in this book, look it up in the dictionary, and make it a word you know from then on.

Words you've never seen before: On every GRE you can expect to see some words you've never seen before. If you've never seen the word in an answer choice, don't eliminate that choice. Focus on the answer choices for which you can define the words.

Your approach to antonyms will vary depending on the type of word that you are dealing with. But you have to be extremely honest with yourself! It's better to be conservative, and to admit that you only "sort of" know a word, than to think you can define a word when you really can't.

## Words You Know

When you are absolutely sure that you know what the stem word means, don't just jump at the first choice that looks right. Avoid careless errors by using the following steps:

- As usual, write down A, B, C, D, E on your scratch paper.

- Cover the answer choices on the screen.

- Write down your own simple opposite for the stem word.

- Uncover the answers and use Process of Elimination: Eliminate the answer choices that are nowhere near your own opposite for the stem word. Then, make opposites for the choices that remain and work backwards to the stem word.

Try this example:

> DISINCLINED:
> ○  notable
> ○  gentle
> ○  willing
> ○  versatile
> ○  robust

Let's assume we can define "disinclined." It means something like "not liking." So our own word for the opposite would be something like "liking."

(A) Does "notable" mean liking? Not really; to be sure, what's the opposite of "notable"? Unknown. Does that mean "disinclined"? Nope.

(B) Does "gentle" mean liking? No. Get rid of it.

(C) Does "willing" mean liking? Maybe. Let's keep it for now.

(D) Does "versatile" mean liking? No. Eliminate.

(E) Does "robust" mean liking? No. So the best answer is (C).

## Words You "Sort of" Know

First of all, you have to admit it to yourself when you're not sure of the word. If you can't think of a dictionary-like definition, but you've seen it before and could probably use it in a sentence, then you "sort of" know it.

### Positive/Negative

Sometimes you can't define a stem word, but you do know whether it has a positive or negative connotation. If the stem word has a positive connotation, its antonym has to be negative, so you can eliminate positive and neutral answer choices. If the stem word is negative, eliminate negative and neutral choices.

Write a + sign down on your scratch paper if the stem word is positive, and a − sign if the stem word is negative. Then, write down + or − next to the A, B, C, D, E you've already written down, depending on whether the corresponding word is positive or negative. Don't forget that you're looking for the opposite of the stem.

Try using positive/negative on this example:

GARISH:
- ◯ adaptable
- ◯ understated
- ◯ explicable
- ◯ generous
- ◯ nonchalant

Let's assume you aren't sure what GARISH means, but that you "sort of" know that it's a negative word. That means the antonym must be positive, which, in turn, means that you can eliminate negative answer choices. That eliminates choice (E). Now turn each choice into its opposite and see what you have:

(A)  not adaptable
(B)  overstated
(C)  inexplicable
(D)  stingy

As you turn each word into its opposite, compare it to the stem word and determine whether it could mean the same thing.

Could GARISH mean not adaptable? Probably not.

Could GARISH mean overstated? Maybe.

Could GARISH mean inexplicable? Maybe.

Could GARISH mean stingy? Probably not.

If no choice presents itself yet, eliminate the least likely choices, one at a time, and try to zero in on ETS's answer. The best answer is (B). Try another one:

DIGRESS:

○ belittle

○ confuse

○ facilitate

○ convince

○ focus

Say you're not sure what DIGRESS means, but you know it's negative. That means the antonym must be positive, which, in turn, means that you can eliminate negative answer choices. Choices (A) and (B) are negative, so get rid of them. Next, make opposites for the remaining choices. "Facilitate" means "to make easier." Could "digress" mean "to make harder"? Maybe. Could "digress" mean "to fail to convince"? Maybe. Could "digress" mean "to lose focus"? That's exactly what it means—maybe your memory would be triggered by now. The best answer is (E).

## Eliminate Choices That Don't Have Opposites

What's the opposite of *chair*? What's the opposite of *flower*? What's the opposite of *philosophy*?

These words have no clear opposites. If they were choices on an antonym question on the GRE, you could cross them out automatically, even if you didn't know the meaning of the stem word. Why? Because if a choice *has no* opposite, the stem word can't possibly *be* its opposite. Here's an example:

EXHUME:

○ breathe

○ inter

○ approve

○ assess

○ facilitate

Let's assume we don't know the meaning of EXHUME. Work through the choices, turning each into its opposite:

(A) Not breathe? Is there really a word for this? There's probably not a direct opposite. Eliminate.

(B) If you don't know this word, don't eliminate it!

(C) Disapprove.

(D) There's no clear opposite. Eliminate.

(E) Make difficult.

You've just improved your guessing odds to one in three. Your chances of finding the best answer now depend on whether narrowing down the choices has made anything click in your minds. The best answer is (B); "inter" means bury, EXHUME means dig up.

## Word Association

Sometimes you're not sure what the stem word means, but you've heard it used with another word or phrase. Use that knowledge to help you eliminate incorrect answer choices. Taking the time to do this may jog your memory of a word's meaning.

DEPLOY:

- ○ relinquish
- ○ convert
- ○ insulate
- ○ concentrate
- ○ deceive

You're not exactly sure what DEPLOY means. However, you've probably heard it used in the phrases "deploy missiles" and "deploy troops." Make opposites for the answer choices and plug them into your phrase.

(A) Does "hold onto missiles" make any sense? Maybe.

(B) Does "remain unchanged missiles" make any sense? Nope.

(C) Does "expose missiles" make any sense? Maybe.

(D) Does "spread out missiles" make any sense? Yes.

(E) Does "remain truthful to missiles" make any sense? Nope.

This technique usually won't eliminate all of the incorrect answer choices, but it can help you narrow them down.

Let's try again:

HEDGE:

○ attack repeatedly
○ risk commitment
○ seek advantage
○ lose pressure
○ become interested

You've probably heard the phrase "to hedge your bets."

(A) There is no direct opposite for "attack repeatedly." Eliminate.

(B) Does "not risk commitment (with) your bets" make sense? Sure. Keep this choice.

(C) Does "not seek advantage (with) your bets" make sense? Maybe.

(D) Does "gain pressure (with) your bets" make sense? Huh? Eliminate.

(E) Does "become uninterested (in) your bets" make sense? Probably not.

Now that we're down to two choices, do you think it's more likely that "to hedge your bets" means to not take risks, or to not seek advantage? The best answer is (B). To hedge a bet is to counterbalance it with other transactions so as to limit risk.

## Secondary Meanings

HEDGE is an example of a word that means something different as a noun than it does as a verb. ETS likes to use the secondary meanings of words—in other words, the meaning of the word that doesn't come to your mind right away. Isn't that just like them? How would you have known that they wanted the verb meaning of HEDGE? You'd have checked the answer choices—if they're all verbs, then so is the stem. Besides, what's the opposite of *a hedge*?

## Combine Techniques

Don't be afraid to combine all of these techniques. Sometimes you can eliminate a couple of choices by using positive/negative, then use word association on the choices that remain. Don't forget to work backward when you are down to two choices.

## Words You've Never Seen Before

Quickly make an opposite for each answer choice. Eliminate any answer choice that doesn't have a clear, direct opposite. Guess the most extreme answer choice you have left. Then move on! Don't spend too much time on words you don't know. Know when to fold 'em.

# TREASURE HUNT: READING COMPREHENSION

# THE COMMON DENOMINATOR

Reading comprehension is the one thing common to almost every standardized test. You've seen it before: a passage about something pretty boring, followed by questions. On the GRE, there are two basic types of passages: science and non-science. The science passages may be either specific or general. Non-science passages will be about either humanities or social studies topics.

## Sample Passage

We will refer again and again to the following sample passage:

It is well known that termites are blind, but little has been discovered about the other sense organs of these insects or their reactions to various stimuli. Body odors, as well as odors related to sex and to colony, certainly play a part in the activities of the termite colony. When specimens of eastern subterranean termites are placed in a jar containing a colony of rotten wood termites from the Pacific Coast, the host termites recognize these foreign insects by differences in odor and eventually kill the invaders. The progress of the chase and kill is very slow, and the larger host termites appear awkward in their efforts to bite and kill their smaller but quicker-moving cousins. Finally, more or less by sheer numbers and by accident, they corner and exterminate the enemy.

Eastern dealated (wingless) termites that manage to survive in the rotten wood termite colony for more than a week, however, are no longer molested. This is noteworthy, because eastern termites of this variety had previously been pursued and killed. Fresh eastern wingless specimens placed in the colony alongside the week-old visitors are immediately attacked, thus indicating that the rotten wood termites have in no way lost their capacity for belligerence.

What else besides odor helps termites interpret the world around them? The insects have sense or "chorodontal" organs located on the antennae, on the bristles, on the base of the mandibles, and on the legs. These organs apparently enable termites to receive vibrations sent through the air, or, more precisely, aid in the reception of stimuli sent through the nest material or through air pockets within the nest material. When alarmed, soldier termites exhibit synchronous, convulsive movements that appear to be a method of communication adapted to the chorodontal organ system, although no sound that is audible to man is produced by these movements. Termite soldiers also strike their heads against wood and other nest materials, producing noises that, after passing through the sounding board formed by the nest material, become rustling and crackling sounds plainly audible to man's duller and possibly differently attuned perceptions. In fact, soldiers of one termite species, found in the arid regions of California, strike their heads against the dry, dead flower stalks of Spanish bayonets and agave plants with such force that the sound produced can be heard several feet away. Other types of soldier termites found in the tropics make audible clicking noises with their jaws.

There is a clear correlation between the functioning of the chorodontal system and termite settlement patterns. Seldom are termites found infesting railroad ties over which there is frequent heavy traffic, or on the woodwork of mill or factory buildings where heavy machinery in motion would cause vibrations. Small-scale tests with a radio speaker and vibrator yielded interesting results when termites were placed in the speaker and exposed to various frequency vibrations. When the vibrations ranged from 50–100 per second, the termites were thrown about; at vibrations of 100–500, termites set their feet and mandibles and held on with all their power; at 2,000–5,000 vibrations per second, the termites crawled about undisturbed.

Most testers read much too slowly and carefully on reading comp, trying to memorize all the details crammed into the passage. When they reach the end of the passage, they often gulp and realize they have no idea what they have just read. They've wasted a lot of time and gotten nothing out of it.

## THE BIG TECHNIQUE: TREASURE HUNT

On the GRE, you read for one reason only: to earn points. The questions test only a tiny fraction of the boring, hard-to-remember details that are packed into each passage. So don't try to read and remember everything in the passage. Treat it like a treasure hunt and just look for the information that answers the questions.

Do this by *not* reading every word of the passage. Just spend a few minutes skimming it, focusing on the first and last sentence of each paragraph of the passage, and noting on your scratch paper the main idea or theme of the passage as a whole, and anything you think is important about the way the information is presented. In other words, case the joint—get familiar with the passage. Quickly.

Don't try to memorize what you're reading, or to learn any of the supporting details. All you should be doing is looking for a general sense of the overall passage which can be reduced to a few simple words and familiarizing yourself with the passage's structure. Remember, the passage isn't going anywhere. It will be on the screen until you answer the question. You don't have to memorize anything.

### Finding the Main Idea: A Test Drive

Try this technique on our sample passage. You should come away with the main idea of "all about termite senses." Scrawl a quick note—"termite senses"—on your scratch paper.

### Attack the Questions

There are two types of questions: specific and general. Because most of the questions you see will be specific, we're going to discuss specific questions first.

### Specific Questions

Specific questions are ones that concern specific details in the passage. You should go back to the passage to find exactly what the passage said for each specific detail question. (See, it's a treasure hunt!) Skim the passage quickly to find where that detail is discussed.

Most specific questions will have what we call a lead word or phrase. These are words or phrases that will be easy to skim for in the passage, such as "The author mentions mayonnaise in order to . . ." (the lead word is "mayonnaise").

## HERE'S WHAT YOU DO

Identify the lead word or phrase in the question. They will be the most descriptive words in the question.

Quickly skim the passage to find that word or phrase.

Scroll so that the lead words are in the middle of the screen. This should put the part of the passage that must be paraphrased to answer the question right next to the answer choices. If this doesn't do it, look for the next occurrence of the lead words and repeat the process.

Read the question again and answer it in your own words, based on the information you found in the passage.

Then use POE.

Some specific questions have line references in them, such as, "The author uses the term 'indigenous labor' (line 40) to mean . . . " Since ETS isn't likely to send you directly to the answer, you should always:

Scroll so that the line number is in the middle of the screen.

Read at least five lines before and five lines after the line number you're referred to. That's where the answer will be.

Read the question again and answer it in your own words, based on the information you found in the passage.

Then use POE.

## POE AND THE ANSWER CHOICES

This is a treasure hunt; in other words: *The answers are in the passage.* Don't pick any extreme answers. Keep everything moderate and stick to the scope of the passage. Don't bring any outside knowledge you might happen to have on the subject. Stay in the world of the passage; that's where you'll find the treasure.

Let's try a question from our sample passage:

It can be inferred from the passage that dealated eastern termites that have survived a week in a rotten wood termite colony are no longer attacked because they

○ have come to resemble the rotten wood termites in most ways

○ no longer have an odor provocative to the rotten wood termites

○ no longer pose a threat to the host colony

○ have learned to resonate at the same frequency as the host group

○ have changed the pattern in which they use their mandibles

"Dealated termites"—those are your lead words. Check the passage—they are first mentioned in the first sentence of the second paragraph. By skimming that paragraph, and a few sentences in the previous one, we see that you're looking for an answer choice that has to do with odor.

(A) This statement is not supported in the passage. While it may be true that the dealated termites have come to resemble the hosts in one way, there is nothing in the passage to suggest that they have come to resemble them in most ways. Eliminate.

(B) This sounds like just what you're looking for. A good possibility.

(C) The foreign termites didn't pose a threat in the first place; all they really did was smell funny. Eliminate.

(D) Making sounds has not yet been mentioned in the passage. Eliminate.

(E) A nutty choice, unsupported by the passage. Eliminate. The best answer is (B).

Try another one:

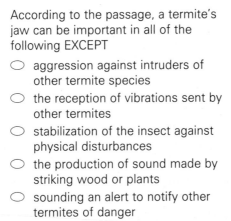

According to the passage, a termite's jaw can be important in all of the following EXCEPT

○ aggression against intruders of other termite species

○ the reception of vibrations sent by other termites

○ stabilization of the insect against physical disturbances

○ the production of sound made by striking wood or plants

○ sounding an alert to notify other termites of danger

On an EXCEPT question, your job is to pick the answer that is incorrect, which means the other four answers are correct and *can* be found in the passage. Keep that in mind.

(A) The first paragraph says that termites kill intruders by biting them. This statement is correct. Eliminate.

(B) The second sentence in the third paragraph says that some of a termite's chorodontal organs are located on its mandibles, or jaws. This statement is correct. Eliminate.

(C) The final sentence of the passage says that termites "set their . . . mandibles" when subjected to certain physical disturbances. This statement is correct. Eliminate.

(D) Termites strike wood and plants with their heads, not their jaws. This statement appears to be incorrect, and therefore a strong possibility.

(E) The final sentence of the third paragraph describes termites making a sound with their jaws. This sentence is part of a discussion of how termites communicate with other termites "when alarmed." This statement is correct. Eliminate. The best answer is (D).

See how we're using the passage to answer the questions? That's because it's a treasure hunt!

Let's try another one:

> It can be inferred from the passage that an insecticide designed to confuse soldier termites would be most effective if it deprived the insect of its
>
> ○ eyes
> ○ ears
> ○ bristles
> ○ wings
> ○ odor

Go back and look for the answer. Soldier termites are mentioned in the third paragraph. Then check the choices.

(A) Termites are blind. Eliminate.

(B) There's no mention of ears in the passage. For all you know, termites don't have them. Eliminate.

(C) Bristles are part of a termite's chorodontal system. A possibility.

(D) No mention of wings, which have nothing to do with senses. Eliminate.

(E) This paragraph just talks about odor. Odorless termites might confuse soldier termites. But why would depriving a soldier termite of its own odor confuse it? (C) seems a better choice.

## General Questions

General questions are ones that ask about the main idea, the theme, or the tone of the passage as a whole. There is no single place in the passage to find the answers to these questions. But the answer is probably on your scratch paper—you've already jotted down your impression of the main idea.

General questions will almost always have general answers. That means that you can eliminate any choice that is too specific (of course you will have A, B, C, D, E written down on your scratch paper for this purpose). Nor will the main idea of a passage ever be something that could not possibly be accomplished in a few short paragraphs. (The author's purpose in writing a 250-word essay could never be "to explain the meaning of life.") The incorrect choices on a question like this will probably be statements that are partly true, or are true of part of the passage but not of the whole thing. Try one, using our termite passage:

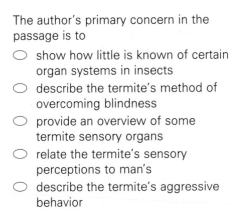

The author's primary concern in the passage is to
- ○ show how little is known of certain organ systems in insects
- ○ describe the termite's method of overcoming blindness
- ○ provide an overview of some termite sensory organs
- ○ relate the termite's sensory perceptions to man's
- ○ describe the termite's aggressive behavior

A "primary concern" is pretty much the same thing as a "main idea" or "main theme" or "author's purpose." Check out each choice without looking back at the passage. Why? Because the details in the passage may lead you astray. The main idea you wrote on your scratch paper should be enough to lead you to the best answer.

(A) Termites are insects, but the passage is not about insects; it is about termites. This choice can be eliminated for that reason alone. If the main purpose of a passage is to describe a particular person or thing, then that particular person or thing will definitely be mentioned specifically in ETS's answer. If you have a passage about Charles Dickens, its main purpose will not be to "discuss the works of English novelists." Similarly, if the main purpose of a passage is to describe something about termites, then on a main idea question you can eliminate any choice that contains no mention of termites. So eliminate this choice.

(B) Common sense alone tells you that termites have no methods of "overcoming blindness." Eliminate.

(C) This corresponds closely with the main idea we discovered. Hang on to this choice. It's a possibility.

(D) We can tell from our quick search for the main idea that the author's primary concern is not a comparison between termites and humans. Eliminate.

(E) This choice makes no mention of senses. The passage touches on fighting, but not as the main idea. Eliminate. The best answer is (C).

# STEP 5
# MATH VOCABULARY: NUMBERS

# IT'S A READING TEST

ETS says that the math section of the GRE tests the "ability to reason quantitatively and to solve problems in a quantitative setting." Translation: It mostly tests how much you remember from the math courses you took in seventh, eighth, and ninth grades. That means good news for you: GRE math is easier than SAT math. As you might know, many people study little or no math in college. If the GRE tested "college-level" math, everyone but math majors would bomb. So, junior high it is. By brushing up on the modest amount of math you need to know for the test, you can significantly increase your GRE math score.

So, ETS is limited to the math that nearly everyone has studied: arithmetic, basic algebra, basic geometry, and basic statistics. There's no calculus (or even precalculus), no trigonometry, and no major-league algebra or geometry. Because of these limitations, ETS has to resort to tricks and traps in order to create hard problems. Even the most difficult GRE math problems are typically based on pretty simple principles; what makes some difficult is that the simple principles are disguised. In a way, this is more of a reading test than a math test. Still, you should brush up on your basic calculation skills, because you can't use a calculator on the GRE.

# THE BIG TECHNIQUE: MATH VOCABULARY

Vocabulary in the math section? Well, if the math section is just a reading test, then in order to understand what you read, you have to know the language, right?

Quick—what's an integer? Is 0 even or odd? How many even prime numbers are there? These terms look familiar, but it's been a while, right? (We've sorted the terms in alphabetical order, but feel free to skip around.) Review the following:

1. **consecutive**—Integers listed in order of increasing value without any integers missing in between. For example: –3, –2, –1, 0, 1, 2, 3.

2. **decimals**—When you're adding or subtracting decimals, just pretend you're dealing with money. Simply line up the decimal points and proceed as you would if the decimal points weren't there.

$$34.500$$
$$87.000$$
$$123.456$$
$$+ \quad 0.980$$
$$245.936$$

Subtraction works the same way:

$$17.66$$
$$- \quad 3.20$$
$$14.46$$

To multiply, just do it as if the decimal points weren't there. Then put the point in afterward, counting the total number of digits to the right of the decimal points in the numbers you are multiplying. Then, place the decimal point in your solution so that you have the same number of digits to the right of it:

$$3.451$$
$$\times \quad 8.9$$
$$30.7139$$

Except for placing the decimal point, we did exactly what we would have done if we had been multiplying 3,451 and 89.

To divide, set up the problem as a fraction, then, move the decimal point in the divisor all the way to the right. You must then move the decimal point in the other number the same number of spaces to the right. For example:

$$\frac{24}{1.25} = \frac{2400}{125} = 19.2$$

3. **difference**—the result of subtraction

4. **digit**—The numbers 0, 1, 2, 3, 4, 5, 6, 7, 8, and 9. Just think of them as the numbers on your phone dial. The number 189.75 has five digits: 1, 8, 9, 7, and 5. Five is the hundredths digit, 7 is the tenths digit, 9 is the units digit, 8 is the tens digit, and 1 is the hundreds digit.

5. **divisible**—Capable of being divided with no remainder. An integer is divisible by 2 if its units digit is divisible by 2. An integer is divisible by 3 if the sum of its digits is divisible by 3. An integer is divisible by 5 if its units digit is either 0 or 5. An integer is divisible by 10 if its units digit is 0.

6. **even/odd**—An even number is any integer that can be divided evenly by 2 (like 4, 8, and 22); any integer is even if its units digit is even. An odd number is any integer that can't be divided evenly by 2 (like 3, 7, and 31); any integer is odd if its units digit is odd. Even + even = even; odd + odd = even; even + odd = odd; even $\times$ even = even; odd $\times$ odd = odd; even $\times$ odd = even. If you're not sure, just put in your own numbers. Don't confuse odd and even with positive and negative. Fractions are neither even nor odd.

7. **exponent**—Exponents are a sort of mathematical shorthand. Instead of writing (2)(2)(2)(2), we can write $2^4$. The little 4 is called an "exponent" and the big 2 is called a "base."

## HERE ARE SOME RULES ABOUT EXPONENTS

Raising a number greater than 1 to a power greater than 1 results in a bigger number. For example, $2^2 = 4$.

Raising a fraction between 0 and 1 to a power greater than 1 results in a smaller number. For example, $(\frac{1}{2})^2 = \frac{1}{4}$.

A negative number raised to an even power becomes positive. For example, $(-2)^2 = 4$.

A negative number raised to an odd power remains negative. For example, $(-2)^3 = -8$.

When you see a number raised to an negative exponent, just put a 1 over it and get rid of the negative sign. For example, $(2)^{-2} = (\frac{1}{2})^2$, which $= \frac{1}{4}$.

You probably won't have to worry about adding or subtracting exponents, but you might be asked to multiply or divide. Just remember this phrase: *When in doubt, expand it out.* In other words:

$2^2 \times 2^4 = (2 \times 2)(2 \times 2 \times 2 \times 2) = 2 \times 2 \times 2 \times 2 \times 2 \times 2 = 2^6$

Same thing with division

$2^6 \div 2^2 = (2 \times 2 \times 2 \times 2 \times 2 \times 2) \div (2 \times 2) = 2 \times 2 \times 2 \times 2 = 2^4$

And don't forget PEMDAS (if you don't remember what PEMDAS is, see number 16):

$(4^5)^2 = (4 \times 4 \times 4 \times 4 \times 4)(4 \times 4 \times 4 \times 4 \times 4) = 4 \times 4 \times 4 \times 4 \times 4 \times 4 \times 4 \times 4 \times 4 \times 4 = 4^{10}$

8. **factor**—$a$ is a factor of $b$ if $b$ can be divided by $a$ without leaving a remainder. For example, 1, 2, 3, 4, 6, and 12 are all factors of 12.

9. **fractions**—A fraction is just shorthand for division. On the GRE, you'll probably be asked to compare, add, subtract, multiply, and divide them. In multiplication, you just go straight across:

$$\frac{4}{5} \times \frac{2}{3} = \frac{8}{15}$$

In division, you multiply by the second fraction's reciprocal; in other words, turn the second fraction upside down. In other words, put its denominator (the bottom number) over its numerator (the top number), then multiply:

$$\frac{4}{5} \div \frac{2}{3} = \frac{4}{5} \times \frac{3}{2} = \frac{12}{10} = \frac{6}{5}$$

If you were asked to compare $\frac{3}{7}$ and $\frac{7}{14}$, all you have to do is multiply diagonally up from each denominator, as shown:

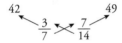

Now, just compare 42 to 49. Because 49 is bigger, that means $\frac{7}{14}$ is the bigger fraction. This technique is called the *Bowtie*. You can also use the Bowtie to add or subtract fractions with different denominators (because to add or subtract, the fractions need the same denominator). Just multiply the denominators of the two fractions, and then multiply diagonally up from each denominator, as shown:

$$\frac{3}{4} + \frac{2}{7} = \frac{3}{4} \nearrow\!\!\!\!\!\searrow \frac{2}{7} = \frac{21}{28} + \frac{8}{28} = \frac{29}{28}$$

$$\frac{3}{4} - \frac{2}{7} = \frac{3}{4} \nearrow\!\!\!\!\!\searrow \frac{2}{7} = \frac{21}{28} - \frac{8}{28} = \frac{13}{28}$$

If the denominators are the same, you don't need the Bowtie. You just keep the same denominator and add or subtract the numerators:

$$\frac{1}{9} + \frac{2}{9} + \frac{4}{9} = \frac{1+2+4}{9} = \frac{7}{9}$$

$$\frac{7}{9} - \frac{4}{9} - \frac{2}{9} = \frac{7-4-2}{9} = \frac{1}{9}$$

10. **integer**—The integers are the "big places" on the number line: –5, –4, –3, –2, –1, 0, 1, 2, 3, 4, 5, 6. Note that fractions, such as $\frac{1}{2}$, are not integers. Neither are decimals.

11. **median**—The middle value in a set of numbers, above and below which lie an equal number of values. Just think "median = middle," as long as the numbers are in order. For example, the median in the set {1, 2, 4, 5, 0, 3, 7} is 3 (put the numbers on order first.)

12. **mode**—The mode is the number or range of numbers in a set that occurs the most frequently. Just think "mode = most." For example, the mode in the set {1, 3, 6, 4, 7, 5, 3, 2, 4, 3} is 3.

13. **multiple**—A multiple of a number is that number multiplied by an integer other than 0. 10, 20, 30, 40, 50, and 60 are all multiples of 10.

14. **order of operations**—Also known as PEMDAS, or Please Excuse My Dear Aunt Sally. Parentheses > Exponents > Multiplication = Division > Addition = Subtraction. This is the order in which the operations are to be performed. For example:

$$10 - (6 - 5) - (3 + 3) - 3 =$$

Start with the parentheses. The expression inside the first pair of parentheses, $6 - 5$, equals 1. The expression inside the second pair equals 6. Now rewrite the problem as follows:

$$10 - 1 - 6 - 3 =$$
$$9 - 6 - 3 =$$
$$3 - 3 =$$
$$= 0$$

Here's another example:

Say you were asked to compare $(3 \times 2)^2$ and $(3) (2^2)$. $(3 \times 2)^2 = 6^2$, or 36, and $(3) (2^2) = 3 \times 4$, or 12.

Note that with multiplication and division, you just go left to right (hence the "=" sign in the description of PEMDAS above). Same with addition and subtraction. In other words, if the only operations you have to perform are multiplication and division, you don't have to do all multiplication first, because they are equivalent operations. Just go left to right.

15. **permutation**—A permutation is an arrangement of things in a definite order. You may remember the word "factorial." Four factorial, or $4! = 4 \times 3 \times 2 \times 1$, which is 24. For example, to figure out how many different ways you could arrange five books on a shelf, you multiply $5 \times 4 \times 3 \times 2 \times 1$, or 120. A *combination* is a permutation in which order doesn't matter.

16. **positive/negative**—Positive integers get bigger as they move away from 0 (6 is bigger than 5); negative integers get smaller as they move away from zero (–6 is smaller than –5).

Positive × positive = positive; negative × negative = positive; positive × negative = negative. Be careful not to confuse positive and negative with odd and even.

17. **prime**—A prime number is a number that is evenly divisible only by itself and by 1. Zero and 1 are not prime numbers, and 2 is the only even prime number. Other prime numbers include 3, 5, 7, 11, and 13 (but there are many more).

18. **probability**—Probability is equal to the outcome you're looking for divided by the total outcomes. If it is impossible for something to happen, the probability of it happening is equal to 0. If something is certain to happen, the probability is equal to 1. If it is possible for something to happen, but not necessary, the probability is between 0 and 1, otherwise known as a fraction. For example, if you flip a coin, what's the probability that it will land on "heads"? One out of two, or $\frac{1}{2}$. What is the probability that it won't land on "heads"? One out of two, or $\frac{1}{2}$. If you flip a coin nine times, what's the probability that the coin will land on "heads" on the tenth flip? One out of two, or $\frac{1}{2}$. Previous flips do not affect anything.

19. **product**—the result of multiplication

20. **quotient**—the result of division

21. **reducing fractions**—To reduce a fraction, "cancel" or cross out factors that are common to both the numerator and the denominator. For example, to reduce $\frac{18}{24}$, just divide both 18 and 24 by the biggest common factor, 6. That leaves you with $\frac{3}{4}$. If you couldn't think of 6, both 18 and 24 are even, so just start cutting them in half (or by thirds) till you can't go any further. And remember—you cannot reduce numbers across an equal sign (=), a plus sign (+), or a minus sign (–).

22. **remainder**—The remainder is the number left over when one integer cannot be divided evenly by another. The remainder is always an integer. Remember grade school math class? It's the number that came after the big "R." For example, the remainder when 7 is divided by 4 is **3** because 4 goes into 7 one time with 3 left over.

23. **square root**—The sign $\sqrt{\ }$ indicates the square root of a number. For example, $\sqrt{2}$ means that something squared equals 2. You can't add or subtract square roots unless they have the same number under the root sign ($\sqrt{2} + \sqrt{3}$ does *not* equal $\sqrt{5}$, but $\sqrt{2} + \sqrt{2} = 2\sqrt{2}$). You can multiply and divide them just like regular integers:

$$\sqrt{2} \times \sqrt{3} = \sqrt{6}$$
$$\sqrt{6} \div \sqrt{3} = \sqrt{2}$$

By the way, here are a few square roots to remember that might come in handy:

$$\sqrt{1} = 1$$
$$\sqrt{2} = 1.4$$
$$\sqrt{3} = 1.7$$
$$\sqrt{4} = 2$$

**Note:** If you're told that $x^2 = 16$, then $x = \pm 4$. You must be especially careful to remember this on quantitative comparison questions. But if you're asked for the value $\sqrt{16}$, you are being asked for the positive root only, so the answer is 4. A square root is always positive.

24. **standard deviation**—The standard deviation of a set is a measure of the set's variation from its mean. You'll rarely, if ever, have to actually calculate it, so just remember this: The bigger the standard deviation, the more widely dispersed the values are. The smaller the standard deviation, the more closely grouped the values in a set are around the mean. For example, the standard deviation of the numbers 6, 0, and 6 is bigger than the standard deviation of the numbers 4, 4, and 4, because 6, 0, and 6 are more widely dispersed than 4, 4, and 4.

25. **sum**—The result of addition.

26. **zero**—An integer that's neither positive nor negative, but is even. The sum of 0 and any other number is that other number; the product of 0 and any other number is 0.

## QUANTITATIVE COMPARISON

There are two question formats on the math section: five-choice problem-solving questions, and four-choice quantitative comparisons (or quant comps). A quant comp is a math question that consists of two quantities, one in Column A and one in Column B. You are to compare the two quantities and choose:

(A) if the quantity in Column A is *always* greater

(B) if the quantity in Column B is *always* greater

(C) if the quantities are *always* equal

(D) if *different* numbers would result in *different* answers

In this book, we're going to phrase the answer choices exactly that way, although on your test it will be slightly different (but it will mean the same thing).

Quant comps have only four answer choices. That's great: A blind guess has one chance in four of being correct. Always write A, B, C, D (but no E) on your scratch paper so you can cross off wrong answer choices as you go. The content of quant comp problems is drawn from the same basic arithmetic, algebra, and geometry concepts that are used on GRE math problems in other formats. In general, then, you'll apply the same techniques that you use on other types of math questions. Still, quant comps do require a few special techniques of their own.

## The Peculiar Behavior of Choice (D)

Any problem containing only numbers must have a single solution. Therefore, the fourth bubble, or choice (D), can be eliminated immediately on all such problems. For example:

| Column A | Column B |
|:--------:|:--------:|
| $\dfrac{2}{3}$ | $\dfrac{3}{4}$ |

- ○ The quantity in Column A is greater.
- ○ The quantity in Column B is greater.
- ○ The two quantities are equal.
- ○ The relationship cannot be determined from the information given.

You know the answer can be determined, so the answer could never be choice (D). So right off the bat, as soon as you see a quant comp that involves only numbers, you can eliminate (D) on your scratch paper. The answer to this one is (B), by the way. Use the Bowtie, so you end up with 8 versus 9.

## It's Not What It *Is*, But Which Is *Bigger*

You don't always have to figure out what the exact values would be in both columns before you compare them. The prime directive is to compare the two columns. Finding ETS's answer frequently is merely a matter of simplifying, reducing, factoring, or unfactoring. For example:

| Column A | Column B |
|:--------:|:--------:|
| $\dfrac{1}{17} + \dfrac{1}{8} + \dfrac{1}{5}$ | $\dfrac{1}{5} + \dfrac{1}{17} + \dfrac{1}{7}$ |

- ○ The quantity in Column A is greater.
- ○ The quantity in Column B is greater.
- ○ The two quantities are equal.
- ○ The relationship cannot be determined from the information given.

The first thing to do is eliminate choice (D), because there are only numbers here. Then, notice that there are fractions in common to both columns; both contain $\frac{1}{17}$ and $\frac{1}{5}$. If the same numbers are in both columns, they can't make a difference to the total quantity. So just cross them off (after copying down the problem on your scratch paper, of course). Now, what's left? In Column A we have $\frac{1}{8}$, and in Column B we have $\frac{1}{7}$. All we have to do now is compare $\frac{1}{8}$ to $\frac{1}{7}$. Use the Bowtie and we get choice (B).

# STEP 6

## DRAW IT YOURSELF: FIGURES

## FIRST, LET'S WARM UP

If there's one type of math that most people don't tend to use in real life, it's geometry. So, first, here's some more math vocabulary for you to bone up on (as usual, the terms are listed alphabetically, but feel free to skip around).

### Line and Angle Stuff

1.  **line**—A line (which can be thought of as a perfectly flat angle) is a 180-degree angle.

2.  **parallel lines**—Lines that never meet. When two parallel lines are cut by a third line, only two different angles are formed: big angles and small angles. All the big angles are equal. All the small angles are equal. The sum of any big and any small angle is always 180 degrees (the sum of the degrees of a line):

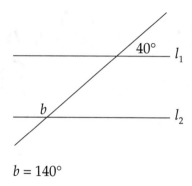

$$b = 140°$$

3.  **perpendicular**—When two lines are perpendicular to each other, their intersection forms four 90-degree angles.

4.  **right angle**—Ninety-degree angles are also called right angles. A right angle on the GRE is identified by a little box at the intersection of the angle's sides:

5. **vertical angles**—Vertical angles are the angles across from each other that are formed by the intersection of lines. Vertical angles are equal.

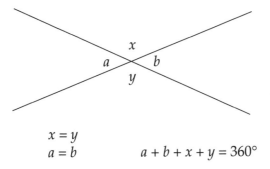

$x = y$
$a = b$ $\qquad$ $a + b + x + y = 360°$

## Triangle Stuff

6. **triangle**—A triangle is any three-sided figure, and contains 180 degrees. The area of any triangle is the height (or "altitude") multiplied by the base, divided by 2 ($A = \frac{1}{2}bh$). Also, in any triangle, the longest side is opposite the largest interior angle, the shortest side is opposite the smallest interior angle, and equal sides are opposite equal angles (see **isosceles triangle**).

7. **equilateral triangle**—An equilateral triangle is one in which all three sides are equal in length. Because the sides are all equal, the angles are all equal, too—they're all 60 degrees. 180 divided by 3 is 60.

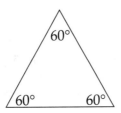

8. **isosceles triangle**—An isosceles triangle is a triangle in which two of the three sides are equal in length. This means that two of the angles are also equal, and that the third angle is not.

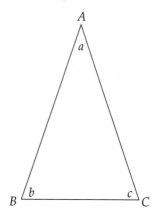

$AB = AC$ and angle $b$ = angle $c$

9. **Pythagorean theorem**—The Pythagorean theorem applies only to right triangles, which are triangles containing one 90-degree angle. The theorem states that in a right triangle, the square of the length of the hypotenuse (the longest side, the side opposite the right angle) equals the sum of the squares of the lengths of the two other sides. In other words, where is the hypotenuse:

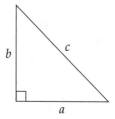

A common right triangle is the 3-4-5 right triangle, because. You might see a multiple of that (such as 6-8-10) as well. The 5-12-13 right triangle also shows up occasionally.

10. **right triangle**—A right triangle is one in which one of the angles is a right angle (a 90-degree angle). The longest side of a right triangle—the side opposite the 90-degree angle—is called the hypotenuse.

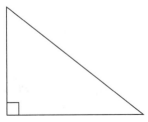

One special right triangle is the isosceles right triangle, or the 45:45:90 (those are its angle measures), in which the two non-hypotenuse sides are equal. The two sides and the hypotenuse have a ratio of 1:1: $\sqrt{2}$. That is, if the length of each short leg is $x$, then the length of the hypotenuse is $x\sqrt{2}$. Here are two examples.

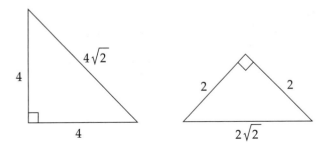

Another special right triangle is the 30:60:90 right triangle. Here's the ratio of its sides.

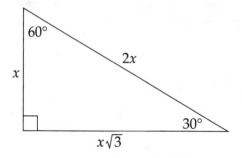

That is, if the shortest side is length $x$, then the hypotenuse is $2x$ and the remaining side is $x\sqrt{3}$. Here are two examples.

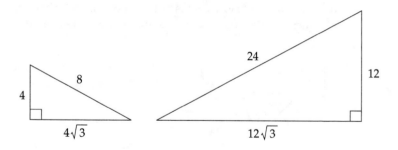

# FOUR-SIDED FIGURE STUFF

11. **four-sided figure**—Any figure with four sides has 360 degrees. That includes rectangles, squares, and parallelograms (four-sided figures made out of two sets of parallel lines).

12. **parallelogram**—A four-sided figure made from two sets of parallel lines. The opposite angles are equal, and the big angle plus the small angle add up to 180 degrees.

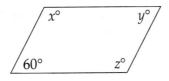

$$x = 120°, y = 60°, z = 120°$$

13. **rectangle**—A four-sided figure where the opposite sides are parallel and all angles are 90 degrees. The area of a rectangle is length times width ($A = lw$).

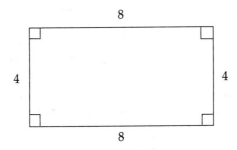

perimeter = $4 + 8 + 4 + 8 = 24$

area = $8 \times 4 = 32$

14. **square**—A square is a rectangle with four equal sides. The area is the length of any side times itself, which is to say, the length of any side squared ($A = s^2$).

## CIRCLE STUFF

15. **arc**—An arc is a section of the outside, or circumference, of a circle. An angle formed by two radii is called a central angle (it comes out to the edge from the center of the circle). There are 360 degrees in a circle, so if there is an arc formed by, say, a 60-degree central angle, and 60 is one-sixth of 360, then the arc formed by this 60-degree central angle will be one-sixth of the circumference of the circle:

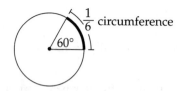

16. **circle**—A circle contains 360 degrees. The area of a circle is $\pi$ times the square of the radius ($A = \pi r^2$).

17. **circumference**—The circumference of a circle is the distance around the outside. Circumference is 2 times $\pi$ times the radius ($2\pi r$), or $\pi$ times the diameter ($\pi d$). For example, if a circle has a radius of 4, and $C = (2\pi r)$, that circle has a circumference of $8\pi$.

18. **diameter**—A straight line segment passing through the center of a circle; also, twice the length of the radius. In this circle, the diameter is 6:

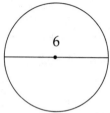

19. **pi ($\pi$)**—Pi ($\pi$) is approximately 3.14; on the GRE CAT, $\pi = 3+$ is a close approximation.

20. **radius**—A line segment that joins the center of a circle with any point on its circumference. In this circle, the radius is 3.

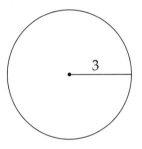

## Miscellaneous Stuff

21. **coordinate geometry**—This involves a grid where the horizontal line is the *x*-axis and the vertical line is the *y*-axis. The *x*-coordinate always comes first, and the *y*-coordinate always comes second.

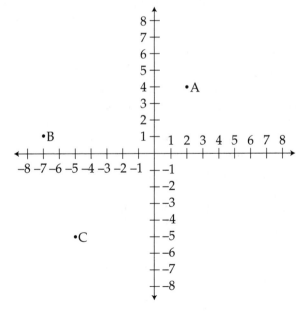

Point A on the diagram above is (2, 4) because the $x$-coordinate is 2 over from the origin (0, 0) and the $y$-coordinate is 4 above the origin. Point B is (–7, 1). Point C is (–5, –5).

22. **inscribed**—A figure is inscribed within another figure if points on the edge of the enclosed figure touch the outer figure.

23. **perimeter**—The perimeter of a rectangle, square, parallelogram, triangle, or any sided figure is the sum of the lengths of the sides:

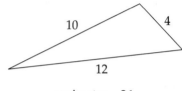

perimeter = 26

24. **slope**—In coordinate geometry, the equation of a line, or slope, is $y = mx + b$, where the $x$ and the $y$ are points on the line, $b$ stands for the "$y$-intercept," or the point at which the line crosses the $y$-axis, and $m$ is the actual slope of the line, or the change in $y$ divided by the change in $x$. **Note:** Sometimes ETS uses an $a$ instead of an $m$.

25. **surface area**—The surface area of a rectangular box is equal to the sum of the areas of all of its sides. In other words, if you had a box whose dimensions were 2 by 3 by 4, there would be two sides that are 2 by 3 (area of 6), two sides that are 3 by 4 (area of 12), and two sides that are 2 by 4 (area of 8). So, the surface area would be 6 + 6 + 12 + 12 + 8 + 8, which is 52.

26. **volume**—The volume of a rectangular solid is $l \times w \times h$ (length times width times height). The volume of a circular cylinder is $\pi r^2$ (the area of the circle that forms the base) times the height (in other words, $\pi r^2 h$).

## The Big Technique: Draw (or Redraw) It Yourself

When ETS doesn't include a drawing with a geometry problem, it usually means that the drawing, if supplied, would make the answer obvious. In that case, you should just draw it yourself. Even if ETS does give you a diagram, if it doesn't match the information given in the problem, redraw the diagram so it does. Here's an example:

Column A | Column B
--- | ---

On a cube, the number of faces that share an edge with any one face. | The number of sides of a square

○ The quantity in Column A is greater.
○ The quantity in Column B is greater.
○ The two quantities are equal.
○ The relationship cannot be determined from the information given.

You're not going to settle for a picture-less geometry question, are you? Just make a quick sketch—something like the following:

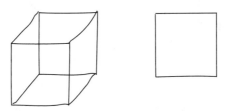

How many faces share an edge with any one face in our drawing of a cube? Looks like each face shares an edge with four other faces. The value of Column A, therefore, is 4. And how about Column B? A square has 4 sides. The values of the two columns are the same. The answer is (C). Isn't it helpful to see the picture?

## Redraw

On quant comp questions, you may need to draw the figure once, eliminate two answer choices, then redraw the figure to try to disprove your first answer in order to see if the answer is (D). Here's an example:

Column A                    Column B

The length of               The length of
the diagonal of             the diagonal of
a rectangle with            a rectangle with
perimeter 20                perimeter 20

○ The quantity in Column A is
  greater.
○ The quantity in Column B is
  greater.
○ The two quantities are equal.
○ The relationship cannot be determined
  from the information given.

So, draw a rectangle with perimeter 16 and one with perimeter 20. It's easiest to make them squares (after all, a square is a rectangle with four equal sides).

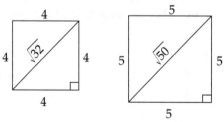

Remember, in quant comp, the answer is not what is in each column, but which is bigger. So just leave Column A as the square root of 32, and Column B as the square root of 50. Which is bigger? Column B. Eliminate choices (A) and (C). Now try to disprove that answer. Let's try to make the diagonal of the rectangle in Column A bigger. Think of "weird" numbers for the sides of the rectangle. How about sides of 1 and 7?

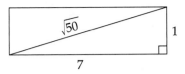

What's the diagonal of this rectangle? It's the square root of 50! So we proved that answer choice (B) isn't *always* correct, and the answer must be (D).

# STEP 7

# BALLPARKING: EQUATIONS I

## MATH SENTENCES?

Many GRE math problems involve words and letters, or variables, such as $n$, $x$, or $y$, in equations. It's time to learn how to deal with those. Before you learn the Big Technique for equations, you need to warm up with some really basic algebra.

### Solving for One Variable

Any equation with one variable can be solved by manipulating the equation. You get the variables on one side of the equation and the numbers on the other side. To do this, you can add, subtract, multiply, or divide both sides of the equation by the same number. Just remember that anything you do to one side of an equation, you have to do to the other side. Be sure to write down every step. Look at a simple example:

$$4x - 3 = 9$$

You can get rid of negatives by adding something to both sides of the equation, just as you can get rid of positives by subtracting something from both sides of the equation.

$$
\begin{array}{r}
4x - 3 = 9 \\
+3 \quad +3 \\
\hline
4x = 12
\end{array}
$$

You may already see that $x = 3$. But don't forget to write down that last step. Divide both sides of the equation by 4.

$$\frac{4x}{4} = \frac{12}{4}$$

$$x = 3$$

## MORE MATH VOCAB

1. **average**—The average (arithmetic mean) of a set of numbers is the sum, or total value, of all the numbers divided by the number of numbers in the set, or $A = \frac{T}{N}$. For example, the average of the set {1, 2, 3, 4, 5, 6, 7} is the total of the numbers (1 + 2 + 3 + 4 + 5 + 6 + 7, or 28) divided by the number of numbers in the set (which is 7). Dividing 28 by 7 gives us 4. So, 4 is the

average of the set. Now, say you were told that Sam's average score for 4 math tests was 80 out of a possible 100. If his scores on 2 of the tests were 65 and 70, what is the lowest that either of his other scores could have been? First, find Sam's total score, using this formula:

$$80 = \frac{T}{4}$$

$$320 = T$$

Now, you know that two of his scores are 65 and 70. Call the other unknown test scores $x$ and $y$.

$$65 + 70 + x + y = 320$$

$$135 + x + y = 320$$

$$x + y = 185$$

The question is, what is the lowest that either of his other scores could have been? Because the tests are only out of a possible 100, and the total of those two test scores is 185, he must have gotten an 85 and a 100. The lower score is 85, so that's the answer.

2. **F.O.I.L.**—F.O.I.L. stands for First, Outer, Inner, Last— the four steps of multiplication when you see two sets of parentheses. Here's an example:

$$(x + 4)(x + 3) = (x + 4)(x + 3)$$

$$= (x \times x) + (x \times 3) + (4 \times x) + (4 \times 3)$$

$$= x^2 + 3x + 4x + 12$$

$$= x^2 + 7x + 12$$

This also works in the opposite direction.

3. **factoring**—If you rewrite the expression $xy + xz$ as $x(y + z)$, you are said to be factoring the original expression. That is, you take the factor common to both terms of the

original expression (*x*) and "pull it out." This gives you a new, "factored" version of the expression you began with. If you rewrite the expression *x*(*y* + *z*) as *xy* + *xz*, you are unfactoring the original expression.

4. **functions**—No, not real mathematical functions. On the GRE, a function is a funny-looking symbol that stands for an operation. For example, say you're told that $m$ @ $n$ is equal to $\frac{m+n}{n-1}$. What's the value of 4 @ 6? Just follow directions: $\frac{4+6}{6-1}$, or $\frac{10}{5}$, or 2. Don't worry that "@" isn't a real mathematical operation; it could have been a "#" or a "&," or any other symbol. The point is, just do what you are told to do.

5. **inequalities**—Here are the symbols you need to know: ≠ means not equal to; > means greater than; < means less than; ≥ means greater than or equal to; ≤ means less than or equal to. You can manipulate any inequality in the same way you can an equation, with one important difference. For example,

$$10 - 5x > 0$$

You can solve this by subtracting 10 from both sides of the equation, and ending up with $-5x > -10$. Now you have to divide both sides by –5.

$$-5x / -5 > -10 / -5$$

With inequalities, any time you multiply or divide by a negative number, you have to flip the sign.

$$x < 2$$

6. **percent**—Percent means "per 100" or "out of 100" or "divided by 100." If your friend finds a dollar and gives you 50 cents, your friend has given you 50 cents out of 100, or $\frac{50}{100}$ of a dollar, or 50 percent of a dollar. When you have to find exact percentages it's much easier if you know how to translate word problems, which lets you express them as equations. Here's a translation "dictionary."

| Word | Translates to |
|---|---|
| percent | /100 (example: 40 percent translates to $\frac{40}{100}$ ) |
| is | = |
| of | × |
| what | any variable $(x, k, b)$ |
| what percent | $\frac{x}{100}$ |

What is 30 percent of 200?

First, translate it, using the "dictionary" above.

$$x = \frac{30}{100} \times 200$$

Now reduce that 100 and 200, and solve for the variable, like this

$$x = 30 \times 2$$

$$x = 60$$

So, 30 percent of 200 is 60.

7. **percent change**—To find a percentage increase or decrease, first, find the difference between the original number and the new number. Then, divide that by the original number, and then multiply the result by 100. In other words.

Percent Change = $\dfrac{\text{Difference}}{\text{Original}} \times 100$

For example, if you had to find the percent decrease from 4 to 3, first, figure out what the difference is. The difference, or decrease, from 4 to 3 is 1. The original number is 4. So,

Percent Change = $\dfrac{\text{Difference}}{\text{Original}} \times 100$

Percent Change = $\dfrac{1}{4} \times 100$

Percent Change = 25

So, the percent decrease from 4 to 3 is 25 percent.

8. **proportion** (see **ratio**)—A proportion takes a given relationship, or ratio, and projects it onto a larger or smaller scale. For example, if 10 baskets contain a total of 50 eggs, how many eggs would 7 baskets contain? Set up a proportion of $\frac{\text{baskets}}{\text{eggs}} = \frac{10}{50} = \frac{7}{x}$. Because you can treat ratios exactly like fractions, you can find the missing element by cross-multiplying.

$$10x \qquad\qquad 350$$
$$\frac{10}{50} \times \frac{7}{x}$$

$$10x = 350$$
$$x = 35$$

Note that we could have made our cross-multiplication simpler by reducing $\frac{10}{50}$ to $\frac{1}{5}$ before cross-multiplying.

9. **quadratic equations**—Three equations that sometimes show up on the GRE. Here they are, in their factored and unfactored forms.

| Factored form | | Unfactored form |
|---|---|---|
| $x^2 - y^2$ | = | $(x + y)(x - y)$ |
| $(x + y)^2$ | = | $x^2 + 2xy + y^2$ |
| $(x - y)^2$ | = | $x^2 - 2xy + y^2$ |

10. **ratio**—Ratios, like fractions, percentages, and decimals, are just another way of representing division. A ratio is an abstract relationship that is always reduced. If there were 14 red marbles and 16 blue marbles in a bowl, the ratio of red to blue marbles in the bowl would be 7:8 (which could also be written as $\frac{7}{8}$). Now, say you were told that at a camp, the ratio of the girls to boys is 5:3. If the camp's total enrollment is 160, how many of the children are boys? A ratio of 5:3 doesn't mean literally 5 girls and 3 boys. It means 8 total parts (because 5 + 3 = 8). To find out how many children are in each "part," we divide the total enrollment by the number of "parts." Dividing 160 by 8 gives us 20. That means each part is 20 children. Three of the parts are boys, which means there are 3 × 20, or 60 boys.

11. **simultaneous equations**—Two algebraic equations that include the same variables. For example, what if you were told that $5x + 4y = 6$ and $4x + 3y = 5$, and asked what $x + y$ equals? To solve a set of simultaneous equations, you can usually either add them together or subtract one from the other (just remember when you subtract that everything you're subtracting needs to be made negative). Here's what we get when we add them:

$$5x + 4y = 6$$
$$\underline{+ \ 4x + 3y = 5}$$
$$9x + 7y = 11$$

A dead end. So, try subtraction.

$$5x + 4y = 6$$
$$\underline{- \ 4x - 3y = -5}$$
$$x + y = 1$$

Eureka. The value of the expression $(x + y)$ is exactly what we're looking for.

# THE BIG TECHNIQUE: BALLPARKING

Say you were asked to find 30 percent of 50. Don't do any math yet. Now let's say that you glance at the answer choices and you see these:

- ○ 5
- ○ 15
- ○ 30
- ○ 80
- ○ 150

Think about it. Whatever 30 percent of 50 is, it must be less than 50, right? So any answer choice greater than 50 can't be right. That means you should eliminate both 80 and 150 right off the bat, without doing any math. You can also eliminate 30, if you think about it. Half, or 50 percent, of 50 is 25, so 30 percent must be less than 25. Congratulations, you've just eliminated three out of five answer choices without doing any math.

What we've just done is known as Ballparking. Ballparking will help you eliminate answer choices and increase your odds of zeroing in on ETS's answer. Remember to eliminate any answer choice that is "out of the ballpark" by crossing them off on your scratch paper (remember, you'll be writing down A, B, C, D, E for each question).

## Charts

Ballparking will also help you on the few chart questions that every GRE math section will have. You should Ballpark whenever you see the word "approximately" in a question, whenever the answer choices are far apart in value, and whenever you start to answer a question and you justifiably say to yourself, "This is going to take a lot of calculation!"

To help you ballpark, here are a few percents and their fractional equivalents:

$$1\% = \frac{1}{100} \qquad\qquad 50\% = \frac{1}{2}$$

$$10\% = \frac{1}{10} \qquad\qquad 60\% = \frac{3}{5}$$

$$20\% = \frac{1}{5} \qquad\qquad 66\frac{2}{3}\% = \frac{2}{3}$$

$$25\% = \frac{1}{4} \qquad\qquad 75\% = \frac{3}{4}$$

$$33\frac{1}{3}\% = \frac{1}{3} \qquad\qquad 80\% = \frac{4}{5}$$

$$40\% = \frac{2}{5} \qquad\qquad 100\% = \frac{1}{1}$$

$$200\% = \frac{2}{1}$$

If, on a chart question, you were asked to find 9.6 percent of 21.4, you could ballpark by using 10 percent as a "friendlier" percentage and 20 as a "friendlier" number. Ten percent of 20 is 2. That's all you need to do to answer most chart questions.

Try out Ballparking on a real chart. Keep in mind that while friends give you charts to display the information they want you to see and to make that information easier to understand, ETS constructs charts to *hide* the information you need to know and to make that information *hard* to understand. So read all titles and small print, to make sure you understand what the charts are conveying.

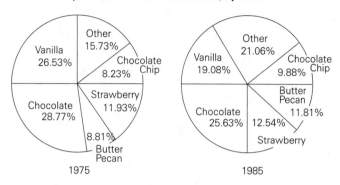

Nationwide survey of ice cream preferences in 1975 and in 1985, by flavor.

1975

1985

Looking over these charts, notice that they are for 1975 and 1985, and that all you know are percentages. There are no total numbers for the survey, and because the percentages are pretty "ugly," you can anticipate doing a lot of Ballparking to answer the questions. Try one:

To the nearest one percent, what percentage decrease in popularity occurred for chocolate from 1975 to 1985?

○  9%
○  10%
○  11%
○  89%
○  90%

First, we need to find the difference between 28.77 (the 1975 figure) and 25.63 (the 1985 figure). The difference is 3.14. Second, notice that ETS has asked for an approximate answer ("to the nearest one percent") which is screaming "Ballpark!" Could 3.14 really be 89 or 90 percent of 28.77? No way; it's closer to the neighborhood of 10 percent. Eliminate choices (D) and (E). Is it exactly 10 percent? No; that means choice B is out. Is it more or less than 10 percent? It's more—exactly 10 percent would be 2.877, and 3.14 is more than 2.877. That means the answer is (C).

Try another one:

> In 1985, if 20 percent of the "other" category is lemon flavor, and 4,212 people surveyed preferred lemon, then how many people were surveyed?
>
> ○ 1,000
> ○ 10,000
> ○ 42,120
> ○ 100,000
> ○ 1,000,000

The first piece of information you have is a percentage of a percentage. The percentage of people who preferred lemon in 1985 is equal to 20 percent of 21.06 percent. Make sure you see that before you go on. Now, notice that the numbers in the answer choices are very widely separated—they aren't consecutive integers. If you can just get in the ballpark, the answer will be obvious.

Rather than try to use 21.06 percent, we'll call it 20 percent. And rather than use 4,212, we'll use 4,000. The question is now: "20 percent of 20 percent of *what* is 4,000?" So, using translation, your equation looks like this:

$$\frac{20}{100} \times \frac{20}{100} \times x = 4,000$$

Do a little reducing.

$$\frac{1}{5} \times \frac{1}{5} \times x = 4,000$$

$$\frac{1}{25} \times x = 4,000$$

$$x = 100,000$$

That's (D).

One more question:

> Which of the following statements can be deduced from the pie graphs?
>
> I.   Both the butter pecan and vanilla percentages increased by more than 33 percent between 1975 and 1985.
>
> II.  A higher percentage of people chose butter pecan and strawberry in 1975 than chose butter pecan and chocolate chip in 1985.
>
> III. The total share of vanilla, chocolate, and strawberry decreased by less than 20 percent from 1975 to 1985.
>
> ○  I only
> ○  II only
> ○  III only
> ○  II and III
> ○  I, II, and III

First, check out Statement I. Did the butter pecan percentage increase by more than 33 percent (one-third)? It increased from 8.81 to 11.81. That's a 3-point increase. Is 3 more than one-third of 8.81? Yes. Okay so far. Now, check vanilla. Vanilla went from 26.53 to 19.08. That's a decrease, not an increase. Statement I isn't true. You can eliminate any choice that has Roman numeral I in it—(A) and (E). Now try Statement II. What's the combined percentage for butter pecan and strawberry in 1975? It's 8.81 plus 11.93, or 20.74. What's the combined percentage for butter pecan and chocolate chip in 1985? It's 11.81 plus 9.88, or 21.69. Statement II is false. You can eliminate choices (B) and (D). No need to check the remaining statement: You're left with (C).

# PLUGGING IN: EQUATIONS II

In the last chapter, you did some simple algebra. It wasn't so bad, was it? But what if you saw something like this?

> Kyle has four fewer toys than Scott, but seven more toys than Jody. If Kyle has $k$ toys, then how many toys do Scott and Jody have together?
>
> ○ $2k + 11$
> ○ $2k + 7$
> ○ $2k + 3$
> ○ $2k - 3$
> ○ $2k - 11$

Tempted to start setting up an equation for algebra? Don't. Numbers are much easier to work with in math than letters, or variables, are. Wouldn't this question be a whole lot easier if you knew what $k$ was?

## THE BIG TECHNIQUE: PLUGGING IN

Let's just take control and decide what $k$ is. Go on—it's okay. "Plug in" a number for $k$. Make it a nice round number, like 10. So now the question reads

> Kyle has four fewer toys than Scott, but seven more toys than Jody. If Kyle has 10 toys, then how many toys do Scott and Jody have together?

Much better, right? Kyle has 10 toys, and he also has four fewer than Scott, so how many does Scott have? Fourteen. Kyle also has seven more toys than Jody, so how many does Jody have? She must have three. And what was the actual question? How many toys do Scott and Jody have together? 14 + 3, or 17. Bingo. The answer to the question is 17. Now, go back the answer choices.

> ○ $2k + 11$
> ○ $2k + 7$
> ○ $2k + 3$
> ○ $2k - 3$
> ○ $2k - 11$

Oh no, there's no 17 here! Yes, there is. You made $k = 10$, remember? Let's follow it through. Every time you see a $k$, make it a 10, like this

(A)  2(10) + 11

(B)  2(10) + 7

(C)  2(10) + 3

(D)  2(10) – 3

(E)  2(10) – 11

Now, work them out:

(A)  2(10) + 11 = 20 + 11 = 31

(B)  2(10) + 7 = 20 + 7 = 27

(C)  2(10) + 3 = 20 + 3 = 23

(D)  2(10) – 3 = 20 – 3 = 17

(E)  2(10) – 11 = 20 – 11 = 9

Is there a 17 in the answer choices now? Yup, choice (D).

Hold on, you're thinking. This can't be. You picked 10 for a reason, right? Nope. In fact, any number will work, and give the same answer. It must. Plugging In makes word problems much less abstract, and much easier to solve.

Here's what you just did, and what you should always do when you see variables in a question or in answer choices.

**Step 1:**  Pick a number for each variable in the problem and *write it down* on your scratch paper.

**Step 2:**  Solve the problem using your numbers, *write your numerical answer and circle it*; that's your "target answer."

**Step 3:**  *Write down the answer choices* and plug your number in for each one to see which one of them equals the solution you found in Step 2.

Even if you think you can do the algebra, plug in instead. Why? Because if you do the algebra and you're wrong, you won't know it because one of ETS's wrong answers will be there waiting for you—that's how they come up with their wrong answers, by figuring out every mistake a tester could make. But if you plug in, and you're wrong, you won't get an answer, and you'll know you're wrong, forcing you to try again. Plugging In is foolproof. Algebra isn't.

Try another one:

If $3a + 4b = 4a - 3b$, then $a =$

○ $-b$
○ $\dfrac{3b}{4}$
○ $b$
○ $6b$
○ $7b$

Two variables? No problem. You need to know what $a$ is. If you knew what $b$ was, it would be much easier to solve for $a$. Decide what $b$ is. We'll make it 5. Plug in 5 every time you see $b$ in the question, this

$$3a + 4b = 4a - 3b$$

becomes this

$$3a + 4(5) = 4a - 3(5)$$

or this

$$3a + 20 = 4a - 15$$

Much easier, right? Now, solve for $a$.

$$3a + 20 = 4a - 15$$
$$\underline{\phantom{3a}+15\phantom{aa}+15\phantom{aaa}}$$
$$3a + 35 = 4a$$
$$\underline{-3a\phantom{aaaaa}-3a\phantom{aaaa}}$$
$$35 = a$$

Okay, now bring in the answer choices.

○ $-b$
○ $\dfrac{3b}{4}$
○ $b$
○ $6b$
○ $7b$

Oh no, there's no 35 here! Yes, there is. Remember, you made $b = 5$. You just have to carry it through. Rewrite the answer choices, plugging in 5 every time you see $b$.

(A)  $-(5)$

(B)  $\dfrac{3(5)}{4} = \dfrac{15}{4}$

(C)  5

(D)  $6(5) = 30$

(E)  $7(5) = 35$

Now do you see 35 in the answer choices? Yup, choice (E).

You should *never* try to solve problems like these by "solving for $x$" or "solving for $y$." Plugging In is much easier and faster, and you'll be less likely to make careless mistakes.

## Good Numbers Make Life Easier

You can plug in any numbers you like, as long as they're consistent with any restrictions stated in the problem. But you'll find the answer faster if you use easy numbers.

What makes a number easy? That depends on the problem. In many cases, smaller numbers are easier to work with than larger numbers. You should avoid plugging in numbers that are used in the question or the answer choices. Also avoid plugging in 0 and 1 in these situations; there's a time and a place for them, because they have special properties. You'll learn more about that later.

Small numbers aren't always best. In a problem involving percentages, for example, 10 and 100 are good numbers to use. In a problem involving minutes or seconds, 30 or 120 may be the easiest number to plug in. Take a look:

> The average test score earned by a group of students is 80. If 40 percent of the students have an average score of 70, what is the average score of the remaining 60 percent?
>
> ○  $70 \frac{1}{3}$
> ○  80
> ○  $86 \frac{2}{3}$
> ○  90
> ○  95

You don't have variables in the answer choices in this case, but there is an important piece of information missing from this problem: the number of students in the group. Just plug one in! Because you're dealing with percentages, 10 is an easy number to work with. So you'll assume that the group contains 10 students. Four of those 10 (40 percent of 10) students have an average score of 70; you're supposed to determine the average score of the remaining 6.

The first thing you need to do (now that you've turned it back into an easy averaging problem) is to find the total. If the average score of 10 students is 80, what's their total score? It's 800. Four of the students have an average score of 70, which means that their total score is 280. What's the total score of the remaining 6 students? It's 800 – 280, or 520. What's their average score (which is what we're looking for)? It's $520 \div 6$, or 86 is $\frac{2}{3}$. That's (C).

## Plugging In the Answer Choices (PITA)

Read this problem:

> Two positive integers, $x$ and $y$, have a difference of 15. If the smaller integer, $y$, is $\frac{5}{8}$ of $x$, then what is the value of $y$?
> ○ 40
> ○ 25
> ○ 20
> ○ 15
> ○ 10

You don't have variables in the answer choices, but you've got them in the question. Because you're being asked for the value of one of the variables, plug in the answers. After all, one of them has to be right. Just remember to write down all the answer choices on your scratch paper so you can cross them out as you go.

When you use PITA, it's usually a good idea to start in the middle and work your way out. Why? Because GRE answer choices are almost always arranged in order of size. You may be able to tell not only that a particular choice is incorrect, but also that it is too big or too small. Sometimes you can eliminate three choices just by trying one. So make $y = 20$, which is choice (C). According to the second sentence of the problem, $y$ is $\frac{5}{8}$ of $x$; in other words, 20 is $\frac{5}{8}$ of $x$.

Rewrite that (a little translation):

$$20 = \frac{5}{8} x$$

Multiply both sides by the reciprocal of $\frac{5}{8}$, which is $\frac{8}{5}$:

$$\left(\frac{8}{5}\right)(20) = \left(\frac{8}{5}\right)\left(\frac{5}{8}\right) x$$

$$32 = x$$

The rest of the problem says that the difference between $x$ and $y$ is 15. Is the difference between 20 and 32 equal to 15? Nope, it's 12. Try again, with a bigger number: choice (B), 25. $y$ is $\frac{5}{8}$ of $x$; in other words, 25 is $\frac{5}{8}$ of $x$. Rewrite that:

$$25 = \frac{5}{8} x$$

Multiply both sides by the reciprocal of $\frac{5}{8}$, which is $\frac{8}{5}$:

$$\left(\frac{8}{5}\right)(25) = \left(\frac{8}{5}\right)\left(\frac{5}{8}\right) x$$

$$40 = x$$

The rest of the problem says that the difference between $x$ and $y$ is 15. Is the difference between 25 and 40 equal to 15? Yes it is. The answer is (B). Why do more work than you have to, when you can just plug in the answer choices?

## Plugging In on "Must Be" Problems

Sometimes you'll be asked which answer choice "must be true." These "algebraic reasoning" problems are much easier to solve by Plugging In than by "reasoning." On these, you will have to plug in more than once in order to find the answer. Here's an example:

The positive difference between the squares of any two consecutive integers must be

○ the square of an integer
○ a multiple of 5
○ an even integer
○ an odd number
○ a prime number

The words "must be" in the question (it also might have said "must always be") tell you that all you need to find in order to eliminate a choice is a single instance in which it doesn't work. So, start by picking two consecutive integers and squaring them. It doesn't matter which consecutive integers you choose. How about 2 and 3? Squaring 2 and 3 gives you 4 and 9. The positive difference between them (9 – 4, as opposed to 4 – 9) is 5. Now read the choices:

(A) Is 5 the square of an integer? No. Eliminate.

(B) Is 5 a multiple of 5? Yes. A possibility.

(C) Is 5 an even integer? No. Eliminate.

(D) Is 5 an odd integer? Yes. A possibility.

(E) Is 5 a prime number? Yes. A possibility.

You've eliminated choices (A) and (C). That's good. It means that with very little effort you've boosted our guessing odds to 1 in 3. But you can do better than that. Pick two more consecutive integers. How about 0 and 1? The squares of 0 and 1 are 0 and 1. The positive difference between them is 1. Now read the remaining choices:

(B) Is 1 a multiple of 5? No. Eliminate.

(D) Is 1 an odd integer? Yes. A possibility.

(E) Is 1 a prime number? No. Eliminate. The answer is (D).

Notice that on the second round of elimination you plugged in "weird" numbers that we usually avoid. That's how you found what would always be true. That leads you to . . .

## Plugging In on Quant Comp

Because answer choice (D) is always an option on quant comps, you always have to make sure it isn't the answer. So Plugging In on quant comps is just like it is on "must be" problems—you have to do it twice. On quant comps, it's not enough to determine whether one quantity is sometimes greater than, less than, or equal to the other; you have to determine whether it *always* is. If different numbers lead to different answers, then the answer is choice (D). Of course, when there are no variables in the problem, the answer cannot be (D), as you learned back in the Numbers chapter. Try it:

Column A | Column B
---|---
$b$ | $\dfrac{1}{b}$

○ The quantity in Column A is greater.
○ The quantity in Column B is greater.
○ The two quantities are equal.
○ The relationship cannot be determined from the information given.

Start by plugging in a nice, easy number for $b$, like 10. That gives us 10 in Column A and $\dfrac{1}{10}$ in Column B. So the answer's (A), right?

Not so fast. You always have to plug in twice on quant comps. The first round gave you (A), which really only means that the answer *cannot* be (B) or (C). Choice (D) is still in the running. The second round of plugging in should involve a "weird" number, a number that you would try to avoid the first time around, something that might shake things up a bit. How about 1? If $b = 1$, you get 1 in Column A and 1 in Column B. That's (C). But you've already gotten rid of (C). Because you plugged in twice, and got different answers each time, the answer must be (D) for "different."

Here's the procedure:

**Step 1:** Write A, B, C, D on your scratch paper.

**Step 2:** Plug in "normal" numbers like 2, 3, 5, or 10.

**Step 3:** Which column is bigger? Cross-out the two choices that you've proved are wrong. Suppose the numbers you plugged in at first made Column A bigger. Which answer choices cannot be correct? (B) and (C). Cross them out! (A) and (D) are still possible choices.

**Step 4:** Now *try* to get a different answer by plugging in weird numbers such as 0, 1, negatives, fractions, or really big numbers. If you get a different result, the answer is (D). If you don't, it's whatever you keep getting.

Why are 0, 1, negatives, fractions, or really big numbers considered "weird" numbers? Because they do weird things. For example:

- 0 times any number is 0
- 1 times any number is the number
- $0^2$ is 0
- $1^2$ is 1
- Any number to the first power is itself
- Fractions get smaller as you raise them to powers
- A negative number squared is positive
- Really big numbers (100, 1,000) can make a really big difference in your answer

## What About Geometry?

On geometry problems, you can plug in values for angles or lengths if the values you plug in don't contradict either the wording of the problem or the laws of geometry (you can't let the interior angles of a triangle add up to anything but 180, for instance). For example:

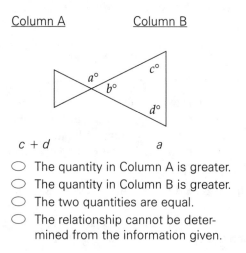

Column A                          Column B

$c + d$                                $a$

○ The quantity in Column A is greater.
○ The quantity in Column B is greater.
○ The two quantities are equal.
○ The relationship cannot be determined from the information given.

Start with the triangle containing angles $b$, $c$, and $d$. Whatever those angles might be separately, together they must add up to 180 degrees. Plug in three numbers that add up to 180, say, $b = 50$, $c = 60$, $d = 70$. Now you can figure out what $a$ would have to be with those numbers; it's on the same line as $b$, and a straight line has 180 degrees. So, if $b$ is 50, $a$ must be 130.

Column A is 60 + 70, or 130. Column B is 130. The answer is (C).

**Note:** In most cases, there's no need to plug in twice on geometry quant comp, since most weird numbers don't work in GRE geometry. (You can't have a negative length!)

*STEP 9*

# STATE YOUR CASE:
# THE ISSUE ESSAY

# FIRST OF ALL, WHAT IS THIS SECTION ALL ABOUT?

And you thought the GRE was all multiple choice! The Analytical Writing section became an official part of the GRE in October 2002, and it's divided into two parts. For each part, you're presented with a topic, or prompt, on which you have to write an essay. The first part lasts 45 minutes and is called "Present Your Perspective on an Issue" (called the Issue Essay in this book), and the second part lasts 30 minutes and is called "Analyze an Argument" (called the Argument Essay in this book).

You should read the directions for each essay prompt. In the past, the directions have been the same on every exam. However, ETS has hinted that the directions might have subtle differences in the near future. Visit the ETS website at **www.gre.org** for a complete list of all the potential essay topics and directions. (Yes, you really get to see this information in advance of the test!) Practice responding to these essay prompts and check to see if different sets of instructions are provided on ETS's website. If so, be sure to mix it up; the prompt/directions pairings you see on the ETS website are not necessarily the duos you will see on the real test. Practicing with a variety of these essays will prepare you for whatever comes your way on test day.

In general, the more writing-intensive the graduate program you are applying to, the more thoroughly you should prepare for the Analytical Writing section of the GRE. However, this doesn't mean that if you're applying for a heavy-duty math program, you should blow off this section. Schools will still see your score, and you certainly don't want to appear unable to write!

## Speaking of Scores

When you get your GRE score back from ETS, you'll receive separate scores for Verbal and Math (on that 200–800 scale) and for the Analytical Writing section (on a scale of 0–6). Of course, you'll be getting your Math and Verbal scores right after you take the test, but since the essays are scored by humans, you'll have to wait to receive your Writing score. Each essay is read by two readers, each of whom will assign a grade from 0 (incomprehensible) to 6 (clear, organized, thoughtfully argued). If the two scores are within a point of each other, they will be averaged. If the spread is more than one point, they'll bring in a third reader.

Your essays will be scored "holistically"—in other words, for their overall impression, rather than the little details or brilliant insights.

This approach makes sense when you realize that each reader, who is likely to be a grad student working part-time for ETS, has a ton of essays to plow through, and about two minutes to devote to each one. Readers will not be looking for spelling and grammar errors (but you should still be careful, of course); they will be looking for a general sense. In other words, they are skimming.

## So What Gets A Good Score?

Research indicates that the essays that typically receive the highest grades, assuming they made reasonably good points addressing the topics given, have one thing in common: length.

That's right, length. So fill up that space! Don't be stingy! Each essay should have at least four indented paragraphs, because that makes an essay look good to a harried, jaded reader. Keep that in mind as you learn more about this section of the GRE.

## How Does the Word Processor Work?

You'll get a very basic word processing program with which to write your essays, so don't fret if you're a computer novice. But brush up on your typing, because you must type these essays!

Here's what your screen will look like during the Analytical Writing section:

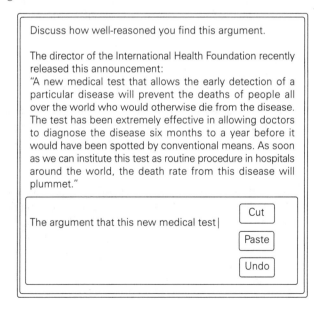

Discuss how well-reasoned you find this argument.

The director of the International Health Foundation recently released this announcement:
"A new medical test that allows the early detection of a particular disease will prevent the deaths of people all over the world who would otherwise die from the disease. The test has been extremely effective in allowing doctors to diagnose the disease six months to a year before it would have been spotted by conventional means. As soon as we can institute this test as routine procedure in hospitals around the world, the death rate from this disease will plummet."

The argument that this new medical test |

Cut

Paste

Undo

The question is at the top of the screen, and your writing area is at the bottom, in a box. When you click inside the box, your cursor will appear. You can use the following computer keys:

**Enter:** moves the cursor to the beginning of the next line

**Backspace:** removes the character to the left of the cursor

**Delete:** removes the character to the right of the cursor

**Arrows:** moves the cursor up, down, to the left, or to the right

**Page Up:** moves the cursor up one page

**Page Down:** moves the cursor down one page

**End:** moves the cursor to the end of the line of type

**Home:** moves the cursor to the beginning of a line of type

In addition to these keyboard commands, you'll also see these three icons on your screen:

**Cut:** Drag your mouse (holding down the mouse button) across all the text you want to move. Then click on the Cut icon. The text you selected will disappear, but it will be stored in the computer's memory.

**Paste:** Use the mouse to move your cursor to the place you'd like to insert the text you've cut, and click the Paste icon. This will cause the text you cut to be inserted at that spot.

**Undo:** If you cut or pasted text inadvertently, use the Undo icon to reverse your most recent action. You can also use undo to remove words you've just typed. (Note: there is no "Redo" button.)

Pretty basic stuff. Note that there is no spelling check function, so be careful; while it's true that ETS readers are not checking for spelling errors, if they see tons of mistakes, they will affect how your essay is scored. So, if you're not sure how to spell a word, use a different one.

Now, on to the Issue Essay.

# THE ISSUE ESSAY

Every Issue topic is a one-sided statement such as "Dogs make better pets than cats because they are friendlier." Well, that's not a real GRE topic, but you get the idea. Your task is to decide whether your essay is going to agree or disagree with this statement, and then, back up your opinion. There is no right or wrong side to choose—just choose the side for which you can write a better essay. You are not expected to have any outside knowledge on any of these topics. You are just expected to make a clear, coherent argument for one side. The most important thing is that the harried essay reader detects a clear, well-argued position. Don't be wishy-washy.

## The Process

Here are some guidelines on attacking the Issue Essay (we'll see them in action in a minute).

1. Read the topic and summarize it in your own words, think about the opposing position, and decide which side you're going to take.

2. Brainstorm. Use your scratch paper to come up with supporting ideas. Jot down whatever pops into your head. Make sure you have at least three to five good supporting ideas. Using these ideas, outline your paper with a template for your final draft (more on this in a bit).

3. Start typing, all the time focusing on taking a clear stand, writing in an organized way, being careful about spelling and grammar, and filling up space.

4. Read it over, proofread, and do some editing. That's why you use Cut and Paste. Fix any spelling and grammar mistakes you notice.

## What Was That About a Template?

If you have a predetermined template of an organized essay in your mind, all you have to do is plug whatever topic they give you into the template on test day. Using a template automatically focuses you. Remember, you don't have to get fancy on this essay. This is not your grad school application essay. This is just a little writing exercise that will be looked at for about two minutes.

Here's an example of a basic essay template:

Paragraph 1: Address both sides of the argument, then, state your position.

Paragraph 2: One supporting idea for your position

Paragraph 3: Another supporting idea for your position

Paragraph 4: Conclusion, restating your position, perhaps with one more supporting idea

Here's another:

Paragraph 1: State your position.

Paragraph 2: Acknowledge arguments in favor of the other side.

Paragraph 3: Shoot down those arguments.

Paragraph 4: Conclude, restating your position.

There are obviously variations on these two templates, but you get the idea. If you go into the test with a structure in your mind, all you'll need to do is apply the topic to this structure.

## Let's Do It

Read a sample Issue Essay topic, and see how easy the template makes it to write.

> Reacting to statistics of increased crime and violence, some have argued that it is necessary for the entertainment industry to police itself by censoring television programs and popular music lyrics. However, civil liberties advocates argue that it has not been demonstrated that watching violence on television or listening to song lyrics depicting violence leads to real violence.

Which do you find more compelling, the call for censorship of entertainment media, or the civil libertarians' response to it? Explain your position, using relevant reasons and/or examples drawn from your own experience, observations, or reading.

First, you have to decide which side of the issue you're going to argue for. Pick the anti-censorship side. You're going to show that the civil libertarians' argument is more compelling.

Now, do some brainstorming: The fact that it has not been demonstrated that watching violence on television or listening to song lyrics depicting violence leads to real violence is an important point. The passage suggests that the entertainment industry police itself, but how? Who in the industry decides what gets censored? Wouldn't the entertainment industry be concerned mainly with sales? And if it were found that violence sells, would they really not allow violence into the market? Also, if we start censoring violence in television shows and song lyrics, what's next? Words that might offend someone? Controversial topics? Where do we draw the line? And who decides what gets censored and what doesn't?

See how this essay could be written using one of the following templates:

Paragraph 1: The issue of censorship is a controversial one. On the one hand, freedom of speech is a tenet of the Constitution, and one of our most treasured freedoms. On the other hand, violence is a serious problem in society that needs to be addressed. However, I believe that the principle of free speech is too important to allow censorship of any kind.

Paragraph 2: (Discuss how watching or listening to violence doesn't make one violent. Give an example.)

Paragraph 3: (Discuss the conflict of interest stemming from the entertainment industry policing itself.)

Paragraph 4: (Discuss the "where do we draw the line" issue.)

Paragraph 5: For all these reasons, I therefore believe that the civil libertarians are right, and that free speech is too precious to allow any kind of censorship.

That's the basic idea, and you have 45 minutes to get it done.

# ASSESS AND ATTACK: THE ARGUMENT ESSAY

# THE ARGUMENT ESSAY

Instead of giving your own point of view like you did with the Issue Essay, the Argument Essay asks you to critique someone else's point of view. You are not asked to give your opinion on the topic of the argument; rather, your job is to evaluate how well the author supported his or her opinion. You'll need to take apart this argument to determine how well it is reasoned. But remember, whether or not you agree with the author's conclusion is irrelevant.

## The Parts of an Argument

A GRE argument is not the kind you have with your sister. It's a paragraph that tries to state a conclusion (a claim or point) with the support of premises (reasons or evidence). For example, in the argument "Vote for me because I will not raise taxes," the conclusion, the thing the author wants you to know or do, is "Vote for me . . ." and the premise, or the reason you should do it, is ". . . because I will not raise taxes."

A quick way to differentiate the premise of an argument from its conclusion is the Why Test. The premises of an argument always answer the question "Why?" In the argument "Vote for me because I will not raise taxes," break down the argument into two parts: "Vote for me" and "I will not raise taxes."

Now, ask why.

"Vote for me." Why? Are we told why? Yes, because "I will not raise taxes." Therefore, "Vote for me" is the conclusion of the argument—it is supported by the "whys," or the premises.

"I will not raise taxes." Why? Are we told why? No. Therefore, "I will not raise taxes" is a premise of the argument, not the conclusion, because premises do not have to be supported—they ARE the support.

## Assumptions

An assumption is an unstated premise in an argument, a statement that would fill an existing gap in the reasoning of an argument. Premises and assumptions are the glue that hold an argument together, and if they're shaky, the argument falls apart.

Read another example:

> Most scientists agree that life requires a planetary
> body. If so, the possibility of extraterrestrial life in our
> galaxy has increased dramatically. Astronomers have

just discovered an enormous number of possible planetary systems in conjunction with nearby stars. There may be millions or even billions of planets in our galaxy alone.

Now, break this argument down. The conclusion is that "the possibility of extraterrestrial life in our galaxy has increased dramatically." Why? Because "astronomers have just discovered an enormous number of possible planetary systems in conjunction with nearby stars."

But isn't there a gap in the reasoning here? Just because something is true about nearby stars, does that mean it is true of our galaxy? The conclusion is therefore a generalization made from a small sample of evidence. To support the argument's conclusion, which is that the belief in the possibility of extraterrestrial life in our galaxy is based on observations of nearby stars, there would have to be some evidence proving that nearby stars are representative of our galaxy as a whole. To attack this argument, you'd pull the rug out from under it by pointing out that nearby stars are not like our galaxy, so the conclusion would fall apart.

## DRILL: SPOT THE ASSUMPTION!

To get you into the GRE Argument mindset, here are a few arguments. Your job is to break them down into conclusion and premise(s) and then . . . spot the assumption(s)! Answers are at the end of this chapter.

1.  *Recent polls taken in May indicate that the third-party candidate for president is already leading the two major-party candidates. Therefore, I'm sure that she will win the election in November.*

    Conclusion: _____

    _____

    Why? (premises) _____

    _____

    What's the assumption? _____

    _____

2. *Ian got good grades in his college courses. Therefore, Ian will probably get good grades in his graduate school courses.*

   Conclusion: _____

   _____

   Why? _____

   _____

   What's the assumption? _____

   _____

3. *Whenever Bob drinks coffee after 10 P.M., he has trouble falling asleep. Therefore, drinking coffee after 10 P.M. causes Bob's insomnia.*

   Conclusion: _____

   _____

   Why? _____

   _____

   What's the assumption?_____

   _____

4. *"The cheating problem has been solved," the university president announced today. "The university will immediately expel any student caught cheating."*

   Conclusion: _____

   _____

   Why? _____

   _____

   What's the assumption?_____

   _____

# THE ESSAY

Remember, in the Argument Essay, your job is to discuss how convincing you find the argument's line of reasoning and the evidence supporting it. You can also suggest how the argument could be made more convincing. Don't be afraid to really critique the argument they give you, but don't give your opinion on the validity of the conclusion (that's the purpose of the Issue Essay). Stick to critiquing the argument at hand.

## The Process

Here are some guidelines on attacking the Argument Essay (we'll see them in action in a minute).

1. Read the argument *skeptically* and locate the conclusion and the premises.

2. Assess whether the argument's premises really did a good job of supporting the conclusion.

3. Brainstorm some assumptions or premises that might have strengthened the argument, and some assumptions that would weaken the argument, and jot them down on your scrap paper.

4. Plug this stuff into a template (more on that in a bit) and start typing, writing in an organized way, being careful about spelling and grammar, and filling up space.

5. Read it over, proofread, and do some editing. That's why you use Cut and Paste. Fix any spelling and grammar mistakes you happen to spot.

## The Argument Essay Template

Writing this essay should be as automatic as possible, because all Arguments are constructed the same way. Here's a practice template you can play around with:

Paragraph 1: "The argument that (restate conclusion) is not logically convincing. This argument ignores certain important assumptions."

Paragraph 2: "First, the argument assumes that (insert faulty assumption and explain)."

Paragraph 3: "Second, the argument never addresses (insert missing or faulty assumption and explain)."

Paragraph 4: "Finally, the argument omits (insert missing or faulty assumption and explain)."

Paragraph 5: "Thus, the argument is not logically sound. The evidence in support of the conclusion (restate the problems with the premises/assumptions)."

Paragraph 6: "The argument might have been strengthened by
(optional) (suggest premises/assumptions that would have better supported the conclusion)."

You don't *have to* stick to this exact structure. But this gives you an idea of what your job is.

Here's another:

Paragraph 1: Restate the argument.

Paragraph 2: Discuss the missing information (assumptions) between the conclusion and the premises.

Paragraph 3: Point out three holes in the reasoning of the argument.

Paragraph 4: Explain how those three holes could be filled up by explicitly stating the missing assumptions.

And another one.

Paragraph 1: Restate the argument, saying that it contains three major flaws.

Paragraph 2: Pick one flaw and state the missing assumption that would fix it.

Paragraph 3: Pick another flaw and state the missing assumption that would fix it.

Paragraph 4: Pick another flaw and state the missing assumption that would fix it.

Paragraph 5: Conclude that because of the three flaws you pointed out, the argument is weak. Perhaps add some suggestions on ways to improve it.

## Let's Do It

Check out a sample Argument Essay topic:

> Politicians should be allowed to get free meals in restaurants, even when they are not conducting official business while eating. After all, the salaries they receive are minimal, and without perks such as free food, we cannot expect the most qualified people to desire to run for public office.

Discuss how logically convincing you find this argument. In explaining your point of view, be sure to analyze the line of reasoning and the use of evidence in the argument. Also discuss what, if anything, would make the argument more sound and persuasive, or would help you to better evaluate its conclusion.

Okay, first, what's the conclusion? That politicians should get free meals. What are the premises, or reasons supporting that conclusion? One is that they don't make that much money from their salaries, and the other is that you won't get the most qualified people running for office unless there are perks to lure them. Pretty shaky reasoning, huh?

Okay, now rip it apart, premise by premise. First, the premise that these politicians don't get big salaries: compared to whom? A local politician might not get paid as much as a high-powered attorney or doctor, but he's not exactly getting minimum wage, either. He can probably afford to feed himself. Plus, if he's chosen a life of public service, he already knows that he won't get a big salary, and must learn to budget himself accordingly. And think about it—wouldn't the idea of a politician you voted for—and whose salary you pay with your tax money—getting free meals really annoy you?

The second premise is that we have to lure the most qualified people to run for office with perks. Isn't the opposite really true? Shouldn't the best people be running because they really want to serve the people, and not because they're getting free stuff? Would you vote for someone who was only in it for the free meals?

Also, the argument states that politicians should get free meals in restaurants, even when they are not conducting official business while eating. You mean, even if he's out with his family on the weekend? What does this have to do with politics? If this were part of the deal of holding an office, wouldn't some people abuse it by going out to the finest, most expensive restaurants whenever possible? And who picks up the tab? The taxpayers?

Is there anything that would help this argument? Maybe if it argued for politicians getting *certain* meals during which business is discussed for free. Or maybe there's another, better reason to give them free meals. For example, if a politician knew he was guaranteed a free meal at a restaurant, he wouldn't try to "negotiate" for one in exchange for certain other "services," such as doing the restaurant owner a zoning favor. In that case, maybe the free meal policy *would* attract better people to run—people who wouldn't be looking to make deals for meals!

Whew! Now that you've brainstormed some ideas, plug them into one of our templates:

Paragraph 1: The argument states that politicians should get free meals in restaurants, regardless of whether they are doing business while eating, is not logically convincing. This argument is based on faulty premises.

Paragraph 2: (Discuss the faulty logic of the "salary" premise.)

Paragraph 3: (Discuss the faulty logic of the "perk" premise.)

Paragraph 4: (Discuss the faulty logic of the any other premise.)

Paragraph 5: Thus, because of the flaws I've enumerated, the argument that politicians should get free meals in restaurants, regardless of whether they are doing business while eating, is illogical and unconvincing.

Paragraph 6: The argument might have been strengthened by (suggest premises/assumptions that would have better supported the conclusion, like the "deals for meals" issue).

That's the basic idea, and you have 30 minutes to get it done.

## SPOT THE ASSUMPTION DRILL ANSWERS

1. The conclusion is that the third-party candidate for president will win the election in November. Why? Because she is leading the two major-party candidates in May. What's being assumed? The assumption is that the polls taken in May are representative of the voter's preferences in November. What's true in May might not be true in November, but the argument

is hanging on the hope that it will be. To trash this argument, you'd show how May and November are two entirely different ballgames in the world of elections.

2.  What's the conclusion? Ian will probably get good grades in his graduate school courses. Why? Because he got good grades in his college courses. What's being assumed? The assumption is that the graduate school courses will be similar to the college courses. In other words, grad school courses are analogous to college courses. To trash this argument, you'd show how grad school courses and college courses can't be compared.

3.  What's the conclusion? That drinking coffee after 10 P.M. causes Bob's insomnia. Why? Because whenever he drinks coffee after 10 P.M., he has trouble falling asleep. What's being assumed? That Bob could not have insomnia for a reason other than the coffee drinking, such as noisy neighbors. Another assumption is that if he *doesn't* drink coffee, he *won't* have trouble falling asleep. Has he tried not drinking coffee to see if that's the case? To trash this argument, you could ask that question, and also bring up possible alternate causes for the insomnia such as the noisy neighbors.

4.  What's the conclusion? The cheating problem has been solved. Why? Because the university will immediately expel any student caught cheating. What's being assumed? The university president is assuming that the threat of immediate expulsion is sufficient to solve the cheating problem. But maybe the cheating students don't expect to get caught, so the threat of expulsion really wouldn't deter them. Also, the university president is jumping the gun by saying the problem has been *solved*. She could say they're hoping to solve it, but not that it's already solved. To trash this argument, you could point these things out, and also mention other ways to solve the cheating problem besides the expulsion threat.

# PART III

# DRILLS

## TIME TO PRACTICE

These drills are divided into sets that correspond with the chapters in the book. Practice the math drills *after* you've read *all* of the math chapters, because some questions corresponding with one chapter might require you to use techniques from another chapter.

Remember, don't do any work in this book. Use scratch paper, just like on test day. Here we go!

## VERBAL

### Analogies

1. CHOREOGRAPHER : DANCE ::
   - ○ connoisseur : art
   - ○ composer : music
   - ○ acrobat : height
   - ○ athlete : contest
   - ○ virtuoso : skill

2. SCOWL : DISPLEASURE ::
   - ○ sing : praise
   - ○ kiss : affection
   - ○ confess : crime
   - ○ irritate : anger
   - ○ hurl : disgust

3. GOGGLES : EYES ::
   - ○ tie : neck
   - ○ gloves : hands
   - ○ elbow : arm
   - ○ braid : hair
   - ○ splint : leg

4. DRAWL : SPEAK ::
   - ○ spurt : expel
   - ○ foster : develop
   - ○ scintillate : flash
   - ○ pare : trim
   - ○ saunter : walk

5. ARBORETUM : TREE ::
   ○ dam : water
   ○ planetarium : star
   ○ apiary : bee
   ○ museum : statue
   ○ forum : speech

6. GALL : IRRITATION ::
   ○ accommodate : deception
   ○ beleaguer : felicity
   ○ awe : apathy
   ○ discomfit : confusion
   ○ inculcate : fear

7. SUBTERFUGE : DECEIVE ::
   ○ decanter : pour
   ○ interview : hire
   ○ account : save
   ○ outpost : protect
   ○ film : view

8. RATIFY : APPROVAL ::
   ○ mutate : change
   ○ pacify : conquest
   ○ duel : combat
   ○ appeal : authority
   ○ tribulate : opinion

9. SOPORIFIC : SLEEP ::
   ○ conductor : electricity
   ○ syncopation : beat
   ○ provocation : debate
   ○ coagulant : blood
   ○ astringent : pucker

10. METTLESOME : COURAGE ::
    ○ audacious : tenacity
    ○ mediocre : originality
    ○ ludicrous : inanity
    ○ dubious : suspiciousness
    ○ altruistic : donation

11. PULCHRITUDINOUS : BEAUTIFUL ::
    ○ ostentatious : wealthy
    ○ intransigent : stubborn
    ○ strenuous : weak
    ○ flamboyant : pallid
    ○ heinous : smelly

12. LIBERTINE : RESTRAINT ::
    ○ litigant : case
    ○ benefactor : generosity
    ○ degenerate : corruption
    ○ pauper : money
    ○ nag : irritation

## Sentence Completions

1. It is the concern of many ecologists that the "greenhouse effect" is changing many of the Earth's _____ weather patterns into _____ systems, unable to be accurately forecast by those who study them.
   ○ predictable . . erratic
   ○ steady . . growing
   ○ uncertain . . uncanny
   ○ chaotic . . unforeseeable
   ○ weighty . . unbounded

2. Children, after more than a generation of television, have become "hasty viewers"; as a result, if the camera lags, the attention of these young viewers _____ .

○ expands
○ starts
○ alternates
○ wanes
○ clarifies

3. Many of the troubles and deficiencies in otherwise thriving foreign enterprises are _____ ignored or diminished by the author of the article in order to _____ the ways in which other businesses might attempt to imitate them.

○ unintentionally . . overstate
○ deliberately . . stress
○ intermittently . . equalize
○ willfully . . confound
○ brilliantly . . illustrate

4. Frequently a copyright holder's property, published articles for example, is reproduced repeatedly in the absence of _____ for its reproduction, an action _____ by long-standing practice.

○ validation . . provoked
○ recognition . . forecast
○ payment . . licensed
○ accommodation . . instigated
○ allowance . . aggravated

5. After screenwriter Neil Jordan's most recent work opened in selected urban areas, many theatergoers were _____, but after pundits expressed their _____, appreciation of the film increased and distribution surged.

○ skeptical . . approbation
○ apathetic . . diffidence
○ ebullient . . trepidation
○ dubious . . disdain
○ unimpressed . . antipathy

6. The pieces exhibited at many university galleries are chosen to reflect the diverse tastes of the academic communities they serve; the curators avoid _____ in favor of _____.

○ continuity . . rigidity
○ variation . . craftsmanship
○ uniformity . . eclecticism
○ modernism . . classics
○ homogeneity . . segmentation

7. The American public venerates medical researchers because the researchers make frequent discoveries of tremendous humanitarian consequence; however, the daily routines of scientists are largely made up of result verification and statistical analysis, making their occupation seem _____.

○ fascinating
○ quotidian
○ recalcitrant
○ experimental
○ amorphous

8. The _____ of early metaphysicians' efforts to decipher the workings of the universe led some later thinkers to question the _____ of man's intellectual capabilities.
   - ○ strain . . roots
   - ○ intent . . superiority
   - ○ intricacy . . realization
   - ○ prevarications . . deceptiveness
   - ○ failings . . adeptness

9. Being gracious should not be mistaken for a _____ characteristic of men's personalities; it is instead a fundamental virtue, one whose very state of being is increasingly _____ by the fashionable directive to "say what you feel."
   - ○ trivial . . imperiled
   - ○ pervading . . undermined
   - ○ frivolous . . averted
   - ○ superior . . renounced
   - ○ immaterial . . influenced

10. While some individuals think that the purpose of sarcastic remarks is to disturb, by turning all communication into _____, other people see sarcastic remarks as a desire for supremacy in miniature over an environment that appears too _____.
    - ○ chaos . . perplexed
    - ○ equivalence . . confused
    - ○ discord . . amiable
    - ○ pandemonium . . disorderly
    - ○ similarity . . upset

11. Known for his ferocious displays of violence and destructiveness, Linker could only be described as ____.
   - ⭘ chivalrous
   - ⭘ frivolous
   - ⭘ callous
   - ⭘ truculent
   - ⭘ repentant

12. Many scholars feel that historical events can be seen as ____; what one group sees as peace-keeping, another group might see as subjugation.
   - ⭘ academic
   - ⭘ portentous
   - ⭘ paradoxical
   - ⭘ trifling
   - ⭘ bellicose

## Antonyms

1. SLUR:
   - ⭘ honor agreements
   - ⭘ settle disputes
   - ⭘ pronounce clearly
   - ⭘ criticize directly
   - ⭘ exclude purposefully

2. MORATORIUM:
   - ⭘ lack of emotion
   - ⭘ discouragement
   - ⭘ savings
   - ⭘ brilliance
   - ⭘ period of activity

3. DIFFUSE:
   - ○ compare
   - ○ chill
   - ○ concentrate
   - ○ blemish
   - ○ oscillate

4. THWART:
   - ○ aid
   - ○ beseech
   - ○ dislocate
   - ○ assign
   - ○ allege

5. AGITATE:
   - ○ relieve
   - ○ satisfy
   - ○ reject
   - ○ condense
   - ○ confirm

6. AUTHENTICATE:
   - ○ sentence
   - ○ disseminate
   - ○ scrutinize
   - ○ theorize
   - ○ discredit

7. ACCLIMATION:
   - ○ alienation
   - ○ adoration
   - ○ facilitation
   - ○ invigoration
   - ○ exaltation

8. TENUOUSLY:
   - ○ having a strong basis
   - ○ following a formal procedure
   - ○ having overall consensus
   - ○ with evil intent
   - ○ under loose supervision

9. FLORID:
   - ○ pallid
   - ○ apid
   - ○ lucid
   - ○ rancid
   - ○ candid

10. MISCIBLE:
    - ○ likely to agree
    - ○ hard to please
    - ○ generous
    - ○ desirable
    - ○ not capable of being mixed

11. PRECOCIOUS:
    - ○ stunted
    - ○ insensitive
    - ○ capricious
    - ○ destructive
    - ○ ignorant

12. PERFIDY:
    - ○ flippancy
    - ○ optimism
    - ○ attitude
    - ○ loyalty
    - ○ humility

## Reading Comprehension

### Questions 1–7

Although the study of women's history has only
been developed as an academic discipline in the last
twenty years, it is not the case that the current wave
of feminist activity is the first in which interest in
5    women's past was manifest. From its very beginnings,
the nineteenth-century English women's movement
sought to expand existing knowledge of the activities and achievements of women in the past. At the
same time, like its American counterpart, the English
10   women's movement had a powerful sense of its own
historic importance and of its relationship to wider
social and political change.

Nowhere is this sense of the historical importance—
and of the historical connections between the women's
15   movement and other social and political developments—more evident than in Ray Strachey's classic
account of the movement, *The Cause*. "The true history
of the Women's Movement," Strachey argues, "is the
whole history of the nineteenth century." The women's
20   movement was part of the broad sweep of liberal and
progressive reform that was transforming society.
Strachey emphasized this connection between the
women's movement and the broader sweep of history
by highlighting the influence of the Enlightenment and
25   the Industrial Revolution on it. The protest made by the
women's movement at the confinement and injustices
faced by women was, in Strachey's view, part of the
liberal attack on traditional prejudices and injustice. This
critique of women's confinement was supplemented
30   by the demand for recognition of women's roles in the
public, particularly the philanthropic realm. Indeed, it
was the criticism of the limitations faced by women on
the one hand, and their establishment of a new public
35   role on the other hand, that provided the core of the
movement, determining also its form: its organization
around campaigns for legal, political, and social reform.

Strachey's analysis was a very illuminating one,
nowhere more so than in her insistence that, despite
40    their differences and even antipathy to each other,
both the radical Mary Wollstonecraft and evangelical
Hannah More need to be seen as forerunners of mid-
Victorian feminism. At the same time, she omitted
some issues that now seem crucial to any discussion
45    of the context of Victorian feminism. Where Strachey
pictured a relatively fixed image of domestic women
throughout the first half of the nineteenth century,
recent historical and literary works suggest that this
image was both complex and unstable. The establish-
50    ment of a separate domestic sphere for women was
but one aspect of the enormous change in sexual
and familial relationships that was occurring from the
late eighteenth through the mid-nineteenth century.
These changes were accompanied by both anxiety
55    and uncertainty and by the constant articulation of
women's duties in a new social world.

1. The primary purpose of the passage is to

   ○ present an overview of the economic
     changes that led to the English wom-
     en's movement

   ○ evaluate a view of the English women's
     movement as presented in a literary
     work

   ○ describe the social and political context
     of the women's movement in England

   ○ offer a novel analysis of England's
     reaction to the women's movement

   ○ profile several of the women who
     were instrumental in the success of
     the English women's movement

2. Which of the following is the best description of Ray Strachey's work, *The Cause?*
   - ⭘ a historical analysis of a social movement
   - ⭘ a critique of an important feminist text
   - ⭘ a feminist revision of accepted history
   - ⭘ a novel written as social commentary
   - ⭘ a treatise on women's issues in the 1900s

3. The passage contains information to answer all of the following questions EXCEPT
   - ⭘ In what respect were the goals of the women's movement in England similar to those of the women's movement in America?
   - ⭘ How were the emphases of the women's movement compatible with the liberal ideals of nineteenth-century England?
   - ⭘ In what way was the political orientation of Mary Wollstonecraft different from that of Ray Strachey?
   - ⭘ By what means did participants in the women's movement in England seek to achieve their goals?
   - ⭘ What historical movements were taking place at the same time as the women's movement in England?

4. The author includes Strachey's claim that "the true history of the Women's Movement . . . is the whole history of the nineteenth century" (lines 17–19) in order to emphasize

   ○ Strachey's belief that the advancement of women's rights was the most significant development of its century

   ○ the importance Strachey attributes to the women's movement in bringing about the Enlightenment

   ○ Strachey's awareness of the interconnection of the women's movement and other societal changes in the 1800s

   ○ Strachey's contention that the women's movement, unlike other social and political developments of the time, actually transformed society

   ○ Strachey's argument that the nineteenth century must play a role in any criticism of the limitations of women

5. While the author acknowledges Strachey's importance in the study of women's history, she faults Strachey for

   ○ focusing her study on the legal and political reform enacted by the women's movement

   ○ oversimplifying her conception of the social condition of women prior to the reforms of the women's movement

   ○ failing to eliminate the anachronistic idea of "women's duty" from her articulation of nineteenth-century feminism

   ○ omitting Mary Wollstonecraft and Hannah More from her discussion of important influences in feminism

   ○ recommending a static and domestic social role for women following the women's movement

6. The author's attitude toward Strachey's analysis is one of
   - ◯ qualified admiration
   - ◯ optimistic enthusiasm
   - ◯ extreme criticism
   - ◯ studied impartiality
   - ◯ intellectual curiosity

7. Which of the following, if true, would most weaken the author's assertion about the similarity between the English and American women's movements?
   - ◯ The English and American women's movements took place in very different sociohistorical climates.
   - ◯ The English women's movement began almost a century before the American women's movement.
   - ◯ The English women's movement excluded men, while the American women's movement did not.
   - ◯ Few members of the English women's movement were aware of the impact it would have on society.
   - ◯ Many participants in the English women's movement continued to perform traditional domestic roles.

## Questions 8–12

Following the discovery in 1895 that malaria is carried by *Anopheles* mosquitoes, governments around the world set out to eradicate those insect vectors. In Europe, the relation between the malarial agent, protozoan blood para-
5 sites of the genus Plasmodium, and the vector mosquito, *Anopheles maculipennis*, seemed at first inconsistent. In some localities the mosquito was abundant but malaria rare or absent, while in others the reverse was true. In 1934 the problem was solved. Entomologists discovered that *A.*
10 *maculipennis* is not a single species but a group of at least seven.

In outward appearance, the adult mosquitoes seem almost identical, but in fact they are marked by a host of distinctive biological traits, some of which prevent them from hybrid-
15 izing. Some of the species distinguished by these traits were found to feed on human blood and thus to carry the malarial parasites. Once identified, the dangerous members of the *A. maculipennis* complex could be targeted and eradicated.

8. Which of the following best expresses the author's main point in the passage above?

○ With the increasing density of the human population, it will become increasingly necessary to reduce populations of other species.

○ Without an understanding of the seven groups of *A. maculipennis* mosquitoes, eradication of malaria will be unlikely.

○ Despite the eradication of large numbers of Plasmodium-carrying mosquitoes, malaria is still a significant problem in certain localities.

○ After establishing the relationship between Plasmodium and the vector mosquito, scientists discovered that *Anopheles* mosquitoes carried malaria.

○ To eradicate an insect disease vector, it is necessary to have a scientific understanding of that vector.

9. Which of the following best describes the reason that scientists were initially perplexed at the discovery that malaria was spread by *Anopheles* mosquitoes?

- ○ Scientists had evidence that malaria was carried by the protozoan blood parasite Plasmodium.
- ○ Scientists felt that because so many species of *Anopheles* existed, they could not be carriers.
- ○ Scientists were unable to find a direct correlation between *Anopheles* density and frequency of malaria occurrence.
- ○ Scientists knew that many species of *Anopheles* mosquito did not feed on human blood.
- ○ Scientists believed that the *Anopheles* mosquito could not be host to the parasite Plasmodium.

10. It can be inferred from the passage that a mosquito becomes a carrier of malaria when

- ○ it ingests the blood of a human being infected with malaria
- ○ it lives in regions where malaria is widespread
- ○ it consumes blood from a protozoan malarial agent
- ○ it has extended contact with other insect vectors
- ○ it is spawned in Plasmodium-infested localities

11. Which of the following discoveries allowed scientists to determine the relationship between the malarial agent, the protozoan blood parasites of the genus Plasmodium, and the *A. maculipennis* mosquito?

○ The protozoan blood parasites of the genus Plasmodium were actually the sole cause of the malaria.

○ The *A. maculipennis* mosquito was found everywhere, but malaria was rarely found.

○ The *A. maculipennis* mosquitoes are all identical to each other.

○ *A. maculipennis* is a group of at least seven species, and not just one, as was originally thought.

○ The dangerous *A. maculipennis* mosquito has finally been eradicated for good.

12. It can be inferred from the passage that

○ blood parasites are all identical to each other

○ not all species of *Anopheles* mosquito cause malaria

○ it is not possible to eradicate the dangerous *A. maculipennis* mosquito

○ malaria is not a very dangerous disease

○ there is no connection between the *Anopheles* mosquito and the protozoan blood parasites of the genus Plasmodium

# MATH

## Numbers

| Column A | Column B |
|----------|----------|
| | |

1. $4[(3 + 3) + 4]$          45

   ○ The quantity in Column A is greater.
   ○ The quantity in Column B is greater.
   ○ The two quantities are equal.
   ○ The relationship cannot be determined
   from the information given.

| Column A | Column B |
|----------|----------|
| | |

2. $\dfrac{8}{9}$          $\dfrac{7}{8}$

   ○ The quantity in Column A is greater.
   ○ The quantity in Column B is greater.
   ○ The two quantities are equal.
   ○ The relationship cannot be determined
   from the information given.

3. What is the remainder when 117 is divided
   by 3?

   ○ The quantity in Column A is greater.
   ○ The quantity in Column B is greater.
   ○ The two quantities are equal.
   ○ The relationship cannot be determined
   from the information given.

| Column A | Column B |
| --- | --- |

4. The units digit in the number 1,743     The hundreds digit in the number 5,243

○ The quantity in Column A is greater.
○ The quantity in Column B is greater.
○ The two quantities are equal.
○ The relationship cannot be determined from the information given.

| Column A | Column B |
| --- | --- |

$$1.3 + .6 + .9 + x = 5$$

5.     $x$             2.3

○ The quantity in Column A is greater.
○ The quantity in Column B is greater.
○ The two quantities are equal.
○ The relationship cannot be determined from the information given.

| Column A | Column B |
| --- | --- |

6.     $4(2^6)$           $6(4^2)$

○ The quantity in Column A is greater.
○ The quantity in Column B is greater.
○ The two quantities are equal.
○ The relationship cannot be determined from the information given.

| Column A | Column B |
| --- | --- |

7. $\sqrt{\dfrac{7}{3}}$ $\qquad$ $\dfrac{1}{3}\sqrt{7}$

○ The quantity in Column A is greater.
○ The quantity in Column B is greater.
○ The two quantities are equal.
○ The relationship cannot be determined from the information given.

| Column A | Column B |
| --- | --- |

Mr. Jones purchased a new bedroom set by using an extended payment plan. The regular price of the set was $900, but on the payment plan he paid $300 up front and 9 monthly payments of $69 each.

8.  $23    The amount Mr. Jones paid in addition to the regular price of the bedroom set

○ The quantity in Column A is greater.
○ The quantity in Column B is greater.
○ The two quantities are equal.
○ The relationship cannot be determined from the information given.

9. Which of the following is NOT an integer if
$K = 21 \times 54 \times 22$?

○ $\dfrac{K}{21}$

○ $\dfrac{K}{27}$

○ $\dfrac{K}{48}$

○ $\dfrac{K}{33}$

○ $\dfrac{K}{63}$

| Column A | Column B |
|---|---|
| 10. $3^{17} + 3^{18}$ | $(4)3^{17}$ |

○ The quantity in Column A is greater.
○ The quantity in Column B is greater.
○ The two quantities are equal.
○ The relationship cannot be determined
from the information given.

| Column A | Column B |
|---|---|

3 is the remainder when $f$ is divided by 9.

6 is the remainder when $g$ is divided by 9.

| | |
|---|---|
| 11.   3 | The remainder when $f + g$ is divided by 6. |

○ The quantity in Column A is greater.
○ The quantity in Column B is greater.
○ The two quantities are equal.
○ The relationship cannot be determined
from the information given.

| Column A | Column B |
| --- | --- |

12. 30      The number of integers
from 15 to −15, inclusive

○ The quantity in Column A is greater.
○ The quantity in Column B is greater.
○ The two quantities are equal.
○ The relationship cannot be determined
from the information given.

## Figures

| Column A | Column B |
| --- | --- |

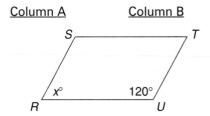

*RSTU* is a parallelogram.

1.    *x*               45

○ The quantity in Column A is greater.
○ The quantity in Column B is greater.
○ The two quantities are equal.
○ The relationship cannot be determined
from the information given.

2. A pie is baked in a circular plate with a radius of 6 inches. If the pie is then cut into eight equal pieces, what would be the area, in square inches, of each slice of the pie?

- ⚪ $\frac{1}{8}\pi$
- ⚪ $\frac{2}{9}\pi$
- ⚪ $\frac{9}{2}\pi$
- ⚪ $6\pi$
- ⚪ $36\pi$

<u>Column A</u>          <u>Column B</u>

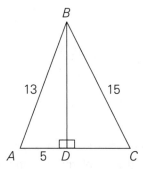

3. The perimeter of      42
   triangle *BCD*

- ⚪ The quantity in Column A is greater.
- ⚪ The quantity in Column B is greater.
- ⚪ The two quantities are equal.
- ⚪ The relationship cannot be determined from the information given.

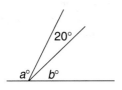

4. In the figure above, what does *b* equal if
   *a* = 3*b*?

   ◯ 40
   ◯ 30
   ◯ 25
   ◯ 20
   ◯ 10

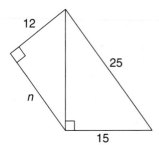

5. What is the value of *n* in the figure above?

   ◯ 9
   ◯ 15
   ◯ 16
   ◯ 12√3
   ◯ 20

6. What is the perimeter, in centimeters, of a rectangular newspaper ad 14 centimeters wide that has the same area as a rectangular newspaper ad 52 centimeters long and 28 centimeters wide?

- ○ 80
- ○ 118
- ○ 160
- ○ 208
- ○ 236

**Column A**                    **Column B**

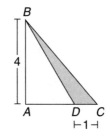

Triangle *ABC* is isosceles.

7. The area of the shaded region in ABC divided by the area of the unshaded region in ABC

$\frac{1}{3}$

- ○ The quantity in Column A is greater.
- ○ The quantity in Column B is greater.
- ○ The two quantities are equal.
- ○ The relationship cannot be determined from the information given.

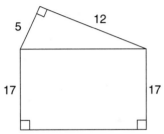

Note: Figure is not drawn to scale.

8.  What is the perimeter of the figure above?
    ○ 51
    ○ 64
    ○ 68
    ○ 77
    ○ 91

**Column A**          **Column B**

The circumference of a circle with a radius
of $\frac{1}{2}$ meter is $C$ meters.

9.      $C$                    4
    ○ The quantity in Column A is greater.
    ○ The quantity in Column B is greater.
    ○ The two quantities are equal.
    ○ The relationship cannot be determined
      from the information given.

| Column A | Column B |
| --- | --- |

10. The circumference of a circular region with radius $r$     The perimeter of a square with side $r$

○ The quantity in Column A is greater.
○ The quantity in Column B is greater.
○ The two quantities are equal.
○ The relationship cannot be determined from the information given.

11. A movie theater is 3 blocks due north of a supermarket and a beauty parlor is 4 blocks due east of the movie theater. How many blocks long is the street that runs directly from the supermarket to the beauty parlor?

○ 2.5
○ 3
○ 4
○ 5
○ 7

12. In a certain machine, a gear makes 12 revolutions per minute. If the circumference of the gear is $3\pi$ inches, approximately how many <u>feet</u> will the gear turn in an hour?

○ 9
○ 108
○ 113
○ 565
○ 6782

# Equations I

<u>Column A</u>      <u>Column B</u>

1. 30 percent of $150    60 percent of $75
   - ◯ The quantity in Column A is greater.
   - ◯ The quantity in Column B is greater.
   - ◯ The two quantities are equal.
   - ◯ The relationship cannot be determined from the information given.

<u>Column A</u>      <u>Column B</u>

The average (arithmetic mean) of two positive integers is equal to 17. Each of the integers is greater than 12.

2. Twice the larger of      44
   the two integers
   - ◯ The quantity in Column A is greater.
   - ◯ The quantity in Column B is greater.
   - ◯ The two quantities are equal.
   - ◯ The relationship cannot be determined from the information given.

3. If the cost of a one-hour telephone call is $7.20, what would be the cost of a ten-minute telephone call at the same rate?
   - ◯ $7.10
   - ◯ $3.60
   - ◯ $1.80
   - ◯ $1.20
   - ◯ $0.72

|          | Column A | Column B |
|----------|----------|----------|

4. The average (arith-   The average (arithmetic mean) of 7,     metic mean) of
   3, 4, and 2           $2a + 5$, $4a$, and 7
   $- 6a$

   ○ The quantity in Column A is greater.
   ○ The quantity in Column B is greater.
   ○ The two quantities are equal.
   ○ The relationship cannot be determined
   from the information given.

|          | Column A | Column B |
|----------|----------|----------|

A discount of 30 percent followed by a
discount of 25 percent would equal a single
discount of $p$ percent.

5.       $p$                    47.5

   ○ The quantity in Column A is greater.
   ○ The quantity in Column B is greater.
   ○ The two quantities are equal.
   ○ The relationship cannot be determined
   from the information given.

6. If $m + n = p$, then $m^2 + 2mn + n^2 =$
   ○ $4p$
   ○ $np - m$
   ○ $p^2$
   ○ $p^2 + 4 (m + p)$
   ○ $p^2 + np + m^2$

7. For all real numbers $x$ and $y$, if
$x * y = x(x - y)$, then $x * (x * y) =$

○ $x^2 - xy$
○ $x^2 - 2xy$
○ $x^3 - x^2 - xy$
○ $x^3 - (xy)^2$
○ $x^2 - x^3 + x^2y$

## Questions 8–10 refer to the following charts.

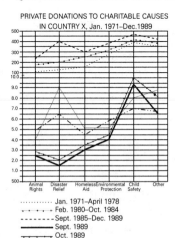

PRIVATE DONATIONS TO CHARITABLE CAUSES
IN COUNTRY X, Jan. 1971–Dec.1989

Private Donations (in millions)

Animal Rights   Disaster Relief   Homeless Aid   Environmental Protection   Child Safety   Other

.............. Jan. 1971–April 1978
.·.·.·.·. Feb. 1980–Oct. 1984
- - - - - - Sept. 1985–Dec. 1989
——— Sept. 1989
.·.·.·.·. Oct. 1989
................... Nov. 1989
.—..—..—. Dec. 1989

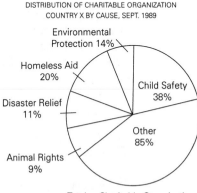

DISTRIBUTION OF CHARITABLE ORGANIZATION
COUNTRY X BY CAUSE, SEPT. 1989

Environmental
Protection 14%

Homeless Aid
20%

Child Safety
38%

Disaster Relief
11%

Other
85%

Animal Rights
9%

Total = Charitable Organizations

8. Which of the following categories of charitable causes received the third-greatest amount in private donations from January 1971 to April 1978?

○ Disaster relief
○ Homeless aid
○ Environmental protection
○ Child safety
○ "Other" causes

9.  If funds contributed to child safety organiza-
    tions in September 1989 were distributed
    evenly to those organizations, approxi-
    mately how much did each charity receive?

    ○  $12,000,000
    ○  $9,400,000
    ○  $2,500,000
    ○   $250,000
    ○    $38,000

10. From September 1985 to December 1989,
    what was the approximate ratio of private
    donations in millions to homeless aid to pri-
    vate donations in millions to animal rights?

    ○  20:9
    ○  3:2
    ○  4:3
    ○  9:7
    ○  6:5

    <u>Column A</u>                    <u>Column B</u>

11. The percent increase        The percent decrease
    increase from 4 to 5        decrease from 5 to 4

    ○  The quantity in Column A is greater.
    ○  The quantity in Column B is greater.
    ○  The two quantities are equal.
    ○  The relationship cannot be determined
       from the information given.

| Column A | Column B |
|---|---|
| 12.    0.01 | $\dfrac{1}{8}\%$ |

○ The quantity in Column A is greater.
○ The quantity in Column B is greater.
○ The two quantities are equal.
○ The relationship cannot be determined from the information given.

## Equations II

1. Alex gave Jonathan $a$ dollars. She gave Gina two dollars more than she gave Jonathan and she gave Louanne three dollars less than she gave Gina. In terms of $a$, how many dollars did Alex give Gina, Jonathan, and Louanne altogether?

○ $\dfrac{a}{3}$
○ $a - 1$
○ $3a$
○ $3a - 1$
○ $3a + 1$

2. If $3x = -2$, then $(3x - 3)^2 =$

○ $-9$
○ $-6$
○ $-1$
○ $25$
○ $36$

3.  Mike bought a used car and had it repainted. If the cost of the paint job was one-fifth of the purchase price of the car, and if the cost of the car and the paint job combined was $4,800, then what was the purchase price of the car?

    ○   $800
    ○   $960
    ○  $3,840
    ○  $4,000
    ○  $4,250

4.  If $x + y = z$ and $x = y$, then all of the following are true EXCEPT

    ○  $2x + 2y = 2z$
    ○  $x - y = 0$
    ○  $x - z = y - z$
    ○  $x = \dfrac{z}{2}$
    ○  $x - y = 2z$

5.  If $x$ and $y$ are integers and $xy$ is an even integer, which of the following must be an odd integer?

    ○  $xy + 5$
    ○  $x + y$
    ○  $\dfrac{x}{y}$
    ○  $4x$
    ○  $7xy$

6. What is the least number *r* for which
   $(3r + 2)(r - 3) = 0$?
   - ○ −3
   - ○ −2
   - ○ $-\frac{2}{3}$
   - ○ $\frac{2}{3}$
   - ○ 3

   | Column A | Column B |
   | --- | --- |

7. $x + 1$          $1 - x$
   - ○ The quantity in Column A is greater.
   - ○ The quantity in Column B is greater.
   - ○ The two quantities are equal.
   - ○ The relationship cannot be determined from the information given.

8. A restaurant owner sold 2 dishes to each of his customers at $4 per dish. At the end of the day, he had taken in $180, which included $20 in tips. How many customers did he serve?
   - ○ 18
   - ○ 20
   - ○ 22
   - ○ 40
   - ○ 44

|Column A|Column B|
|---|---|

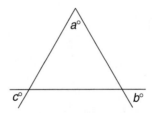

9.  $b + c$                      $180 - a$

○ The quantity in Column A is greater.
○ The quantity in Column B is greater.
○ The two quantities are equal.
○ The relationship cannot be determined from the information given.

10. In a certain election, 60 percent of the voters were women. If 30 percent of the women and 20 percent of the men voted for candidate X, what percent of all the voters in that election voted for candidate X?

○ 18%
○ 25%
○ 26%
○ 30%
○ 50%

| Column A | Column B |
| --- | --- |

11.  $xy$ $\qquad\qquad\qquad$ $x\sqrt{y}$

- ○ The quantity in Column A is greater.
- ○ The quantity in Column B is greater.
- ○ The two quantities are equal.
- ○ The relationship cannot be determined from the information given.

12. The units digit of a 2-digit number is 3 times the tens digit. If the digits are reversed, the resulting number is 36 more than the original number. What is the original number?

- ○ 13
- ○ 26
- ○ 36
- ○ 62
- ○ 93

PART **IV**

# ANSWERS AND EXPLANATIONS

## VERBAL

### Analogies

1. **B**    Make a sentence: A CHOREOGRAPHER creates a DANCE.
   (A) Does a connoisseur create art? Nope.
   (B) Does a composer create music? Yes.
   (C) Does an acrobat create height? Nope.
   (D) Does an athlete create contest? Nope.
   (E) Does a virtuoso create skill? She has it, but she doesn't create it. (B) is best.

2. **B**    Make a sentence: To SCOWL means to show DISPLEASURE. The only answer choice that fits this sentence is choice (B): To kiss means to show affection.

3. **B**    Make a sentence: GOGGLES provide protection for the EYES. The only answer choice that fits this sentence is (B): Gloves provide protection for the hands.

4. **E**    Make a sentence: To DRAWL means to SPEAK slowly. Answer choices (A), (B), and (D) don't fit this sentence. If you weren't sure of the meaning of "scintillate," ask yourself, "Could it mean to flash slowly?" Not likely. And "saunter" does mean to walk slowly. That's (E). Now look up "scintillate."

5. **C**    If you're not exactly sure what ARBORETUM means, work backward. Make a sentence for each answer choice and see whether the stem words would fit that sentence.
   (A) You could say "A dam holds back the flow of water." Could something hold back the flow of a TREE? No way.
   (B) You might say, "A planetarium is a room where the image of a star is projected." Could something be a room where the image of a TREE is projected? Not likely.
   (C) Perhaps you're not sure what an apiary is—never eliminate an answer choice when you don't know the meaning of one of the words. (By the way, it's a collection of bee hives.)
   (D) You might be thinking, "A museum is a place to exhibit a statue, " but lots of things are exhibited in a museum besides statues, and statues can be found lots of other places. This one is kind of weak, and should probably be eliminated.

(E) Your sentence might be "A forum is a public place where a person makes a speech." Could something be a public place where a person makes a TREE? No chance. The best answer is (C). And a good sentence for the stem words is "An ARBORETUM is a man-made environment where a TREE grows."

6. **D**    If you're not sure what GALL means, go right to the answers. Choices (A), (B), (C), and (E) all contain words that are not related to each other, but you'd have to leave in any choices containing words you don't know. In (D), "discomfit" means to cause confusion, and GALL means to cause IRRITATION. Bingo!

7. **A**    If you're not sure what a SUBTERFUGE is, go right to the answers and eliminate choices. In (A), are "decanter" and "pour" related? Yes, the function of a decanter is to pour. Could the function of a SUBTERFUGE be to DECEIVE? Sure. Keep this choice. In (B), are "hire" and "interview" related? Try making a sentence . . . no. Eliminate this choice. In (C), are "account" and "save" related? No. Yes, there are such things as "savings accounts," but the words "save" and "account" do not have a relationship to each other (remember, we need *dictionary definitions* in our relationships). Eliminate this choice. In (D), are "outpost" and "protect" related? Not really. Some outposts might be used for protection, but an outpost is really just an outlying settlement. "Protect" is not in the definition of "outpost." Eliminate this choice. In (E), are "film" and "view" related? No. Many other things are viewed besides a film (remember, we need *dictionary definitions* in our relationships). Eliminate this choice. The only answer left is (A), and yes, the function of a SUBTERFUGE is to DECEIVE. That is its *definition*.

8. **C**    If you're not sure what RATIFY means, go right to the answers and eliminate choices. Choices (B) and (D) contain words that aren't related to each other. Work backward on choices (A) and (C): "To mutate is to make a change in nature or form." Could RATIFY mean to make an APPROVAL in nature or form? Not likely. For choice (C), "To duel is to have a formal combat, according to rules." Could to RATIFY mean to have a formal APPROVAL, according to rules? Yes!

9.  **E**  SOPORIFIC is a word you need to know for the GRE—ETS loves it. Something soporific causes sleep. That sentence eliminates answer choices (A), (B), (C), and (D). Something astringent does cause a pucker.

10. **C**  If you don't know what METTLESOME means, go right to the answer choices and start eliminating. Answer choices (A), (B), and (E) contain words that are not related to each other, so eliminate them. Then make sentences for the remaining answer choices, and work backward to the stem words. For answer choice (C), your sentence would be "Something ludicrous is characterized by inanity." Could something METTLESOME be characterized by COURAGE? Sure. For choice (D), your sentence would be "Something dubious causes suspiciousness." Could something METTLESOME cause COURAGE? Does *anything* cause COURAGE? Not really.

11. **B**  If you don't know what PULCHRITUDINOUS means, go to the answers. (A) Are ostentatious and wealthy related? Not necessarily—ostentatious means showing off, but you can be ostentatious about knowledge too. (B)Are intransigent and stubborn related? If you're not sure, leave it in, but intransigent means extremely stubborn. Could something mean extremely BEAUTIFUL? Sure. (C) Are strenuous and weak related? Well, strenuous means something that requires great effort, and if you're weak, you'd have trouble with something like that, but you can't really define the word strenuous with the word weak. Eliminate it. (D) Are flamboyant and pallid related? If you're not sure, leave it in, but flamboyant means showy or elaborate, and pallid means extremely pale. You might think they're opposites, but try making a sentence: someone flamboyant is not pallid? Not necessarily—you could be extremely pale and still be showy. Eliminate it. (E) Are heinous and smelly related? If you're not sure, leave it in, but heinous means really horrible and wicked, which wouldn't really describe a smell, no matter how bad. The best answer is (B).

12. **D**  Not sure about LIBERTINE? Go to the answers. (A) Are litigant and case related? Sort of; a litigant brings a case to court. Could a LIBERTINE bring a RESTRAINT to court? Doesn't make sense, so get rid of it. (B) Are benefactor and generosity related? Yes, a benefactor has generosity. Could

a LIBERTINE have RESTRAINT? Maybe. Keep it. (C) Are degenerate and corruption related? Yes, a degenerate has corruption. But that's the same relationship as the one in B, so neither of them could be the answer, because (B) and (C) cancel each other out. (D) Are pauper and money related? Yes, a pauper has no money. Could a LIBERTINE have no RESTRAINT? Maybe. Are nag and irritation related? Yes, a nag causes irritation. Could a LIBERTINE cause RESTRAINT? To "cause restraint" doesn't really make sense. The best answer is (D).

## Sentence Completions

1. **A**    Focus on the second blank. The clue for the second blank is "unable to be accurately forecast." So a good word for the second blank would be "unpredictable." Looking at the second answer-choice words only, that eliminates answer choices (B) and (E). The clue for the first blank is "changing," so the first blank must be a word that's the opposite of the one for the second blank, or "predictable." That eliminates answer choices (C) and (D) and leaves you with (A).

2. **D**    The clue in the sentence is "Children . . . have become 'hasty viewers.'" The trigger punctuation is a "same-direction" semi-colon. So a good word for the blank would be "wanders." In any case, it has to be a negative word. The words in answer choices (A), (B), and (E) are positive, and answer choice (C) isn't really negative. That leaves (D).

3. **B**    The clue for the second blank is "the ways in which other businesses might attempt to imitate them." The trigger words are "in order to." So a good word for the second blank would be "highlight." That eliminates answer choices (A), (C), and (D). The clue for the first blank is "the troubles and deficiencies . . . ignored or diminished by the author . . ." So a good word for the first blank would be "intentionally." That eliminates answer choice (E) and leaves (B).

4. **C**    The clue for the second blank is "reproduced repeatedly . . . by long-standing practice." A good word for the second blank would be "approved." Looking only at the second words in the answer choices, you can eliminate answer choices (A), (B), (D), and (E).

5. **A** The clue for the second blank is "appreciation of the film increased," so the word in the second blank must be positive. Looking only at the second words in the answer choices, you can eliminate answer choices (B), (C), (D), and (E), because the second words in all these choices are negative. Or, if you weren't sure about the second words, you know the first word has to be negative because of the trigger word "but." That eliminates (C) and (E).

6. **C** The clue in the sentence is "diverse tastes," so put "diversity" in the second blank. That eliminates (A), (B), (D), and (E). It's (C).

7. **B** The clue for the blank after the trigger word "however" is "daily routines," so the word in the blank can be "routine." That definitely eliminates (A), (D), and (E). If you know what "quotidian" or "recalcitrant" means, you know the answer is (B). If you don't, (C) is a good guess (although it's wrong).

8. **E** The clue in the sentence is "led some later thinkers to question." That tells you that there was some problem with the "early metaphysicians' efforts to decipher the workings of the universe." So a good word for the first blank would be "problems." That eliminates answer choices (A), (B), and (C). The second blank must be a word such as "workings," or at least one with positive connotations. That eliminates answer choice (D) and leaves you with (E).

9. **A** The clue in the sentence is "Being gracious . . . is instead a fundamental virtue." This tells you that the word in the first blank means the opposite of "fundamental virtue," or at least is one with negative connotations. That eliminates answer choices (B), (C), and (D). The virtue of being gracious would be "threatened" by "the fashionable directive to 'say what you feel.'" That eliminates answer choice (E) and leaves (A).

10. **D** The clue for the first blank is "the purpose of sarcastic remarks is to disturb." So a good word for the first blank would be "disturbances." That eliminates answer choices (B) and (E). The clue for the second blank is "desire for supremacy in miniature over an environment." So a word for how that environment appears must have negative

connotations. That eliminates answer choice (A) (perplexed is negative, but an "environment" can't really appear "perplexed") and (C). You're left with (D).

11. **D**  The clue is "ferocious displays of violence and destructiveness." We're looking for a word for the blank that means "ferocious displays of violence and destructiveness"; just shorten that to violent. It's all about vocabulary now. (A) Chivalrous means polite and gallant, so eliminate it. (B) Frivolous means silly or trivial, so eliminate it. (C) Callous means unfeeling, but that's not the same as violent, so eliminate it. (D) Truculent means violent and destructive; sounds good. (E) Repentant means apologetic, so eliminate it. The best answer is (D).

12. **C**  That semicolon is a trigger punctuation. It tells you that the first part of the sentence agrees with the second part. The second part contains the clue "what one group sees as peacekeeping, another group might see as subjugation." How can we describe that—it sounds like a contradiction. How about "contradictory" for the blank? Time to go to the answers. You can eliminate (A) academic, because it doesn't mean contradictory. (B) portentous means predicting the future, which might be true of historical events, but has nothing to do with this sentence. (C) paradoxical means seemingly contradictory, so keep it (if you weren't sure, you'd keep it in anyway). (D) trifling means frivolous or of little value, so eliminate it. (E) bellicose means warlike, which might be true of some historical events, but has nothing to do with this sentence. The best answer is (C).

## Antonyms

1. **C**  SLUR means to pronounce indistinctly.

2. **E**  A MORATORIUM is a period of inactivity.

3. **C**  DIFFUSE means to spread out, or disperse.

4. **A**  THWART means to prevent from taking place, or to frustrate.

5. **A**  AGITATE means to upset or disturb.

6. **E**  AUTHENTICATE means to establish as being genuine.

7. **A** ACCLIMATION means an adjustment to a new environment or situation. It's a word with positive connotations, so you could eliminate answer choices that have positive connotations (the opposite of "acclimation" must be a negative word). Answer choices (B), (C), (D), and (E) are all positive words, so they're gone.

8. **A** TENUOUS means insubstantial or flimsy. If you knew only that it was negative, you could eliminate answer choices with negative connotations, like (D) and (E) for sure, and (B) too.

9. **A** FLORID means flushed with rosy color. If you knew only that it was positive, you could eliminate answer choices (C) and (E), which are positive words. Answer choices (B) and (D) would be good guesses.

10. **E** MISCIBLE means able to be mixed. Hey, it's a tough one. If you don't know the word, just guess and move on.

11. **A** PRECOCIOUS means characterized by unusually early development or maturity, especially in mental abilities. The opposite would be something like "undeveloped." Choice (A), stunted, means undeveloped. That looks correct.

12. **D** PERFIDY means treachery. Maybe all you knew is it was a negative word. That would at least eliminate negative and neutral words, like choices (A) and (C).

## Reading Comprehension

1. **C** This is a main idea question about the passage as a whole. Your "treasure hunt" should have revealed that the passage is basically discussing the way in which Strachey interprets the English women's movement. Eliminate (B) right away because it's not about a "literary" work. Eliminate (D) because it's not a "novel analysis." Eliminate (A) and (E) because they are too specific. That leaves (C).

2. **A** Go back to the second paragraph where the book is described. From the first sentence, you know it's about "the historical connections between the women's movement and other social and political developments." Sounds like (A).

3. **C** Because this is an EXCEPT question, you're looking for the choice that the passage does not answer. The passage

discussed how Wollstonecraft's political orientation differed from More's, but not how it differed from Strachey's. That's (C).

4. **C**    For line reference questions, go back to the lines cited, and read about five lines before and after those lines. You can find the answer in either place for this question. The first sentence of the paragraph tells us Strachey is writing about "the historical connections between the women's movement and other social and political developments." Choice (C) is just a paraphrase of this.

5. **B**    Look back in the passage for the place where the author "faults" Strachey. It's in the last paragraph, in lines 46–50. The author states, "Where Strachey pictured a relatively fixed image of domestic women throughout the first half of the nineteenth century, recent historical and literary works suggest that this image was both complex and unstable." Sounds like (B).

6. **A**    The author likes Strachey's book, but points out something that Strachey omitted. The attitude is positive, but not overly positive. That's (A). Make sure you know the meaning of the word "qualified" as it's used in this context.

7. **D**    First, go back to the passage to find out what the author said about "the similarity between the English and American women's movements." It's at the end of the first paragraph. The author says that "like its American counterpart, the English women's movement had a powerful sense of its own historic importance and of its relationship to wider social and political change." So you're looking for an answer choice that would indicate that was not true. Choice (D) directly contradicts the author's assertion.

8. **E**    This is a main idea question, about the passage as a whole. Your "treasure hunt" should have revealed that the passage is about how scientists study insects that carry malaria so that those insects could be eradicated. (A) doesn't even mention insects. (C) doesn't mention how scientists study the bugs. (D) doesn't mention eradicating the insects. Because there's no prediction of the future, you can eliminate (B). That leaves (E).

9. **C** Go back to the first paragraph. In lines 7–8 the passage states, "In some localities the mosquito was abundant but malaria rare or absent."

10. **A** Reread the second sentence of the second paragraph. It says that the mosquito becomes a carrier when it feeds on human blood.

11. **D** Around line 10 of the passage, it says that the problem of the relationship between all of these things had been solved in 1934, when it was discovered that "*A. maculipennis* is not a single species but a group of at least seven."

12. **B** The passage says that at first, scientists were confused because sometimes the *Anopheles* mosquito was present, but the malaria was not, and sometimes the malaria was present and the mosquito was not. Then, they discovered that *A. maculipennis* is a group of at least seven species, and not just one, as was originally thought. That would explain the discrepancy—it must be true that not all species of *Anopheles* mosquito cause malaria, just certain ones.

## MATH

### Numbers

1. **B** First, eliminate (D) because you're only working with numbers here. Don't forget the order of operations, or PEMDAS. Add 3 + 3 in the inner parentheses first; you get 4[6 + 4]. Now, do the remaining set of parentheses; you will get this: 4[10], or 40. So, in Column A, you have 40, and in Column B you have 45. The answer is (B).

2. **A** First, eliminate (D) because you're only working with numbers here. All you have to do here is use the Bowtie to compare these fractions. You end up comparing 64 (in Column A) and 63 (in Column B). The answer is (A).

3. **E** Remember the quick test to tell whether a number is divisible by 3? Add up the digits in the number. 1 + 1 + 7 = 9, and, because 9 is divisible by 3, 117 is too. Also, because 117 is divisible by 3, there will be no remainder, so the answer is (E).

4. **A** The units digit in 1,743 is 3. The hundreds digit in 5,243 is 2. The answer is (A).

5. **B** Add the decimals: $1.3 + 0.6 + 0.9 = 2.8$. So, $2.8 + x = 5$. Now, $5 - 2.8$ is $2.2$, so $x = 2.2$. Column A is $2.2$, and Column B is $2.3$, so the answer is (B).

6. **A** When in doubt, expand it out, and don't calculate, because this is quant comp and you only have to compare. In Column A, there is $(4)(2)(2)(2)(2)(2)(2)$. In Column B, there is $(6)(4)(4)$. Break it down even further: Column A is $(2)(2)(2)(2)(2)(2)(2)(2)$, and Column B is $(3)(2)(2)(2)(2)(2)$. Now, get rid of anything both columns have in common. Each column has five 2s, so cross them out. What's left? $(2)(2)(2)$ in Column A and $(3)$ in Column B. In other words, Column A has an 8, and Column B has a 3. The answer is (A).

7. **A** What would happen if we squared both values? We'd get $\frac{7}{3}$ in Column A and $\frac{1}{9}$ (7) in Column B. Which is bigger, $\frac{7}{3}$ or $\frac{7}{9}$? $\frac{7}{3}$ because it's more than 1 (if you're not sure, use the Bowtie to compare them). The answer is (A).

8. **A** To find the amount Mr. Jones paid in addition to the regular price of the bedroom set, multiply $69 by the 9 months and get $621. Then add the $300 payment. $621 + 300 = 921$. So Mr. Jones paid an additional $21. The $23 in Column A is larger than the $21 in Column B. The answer is (A).

9. **C** You don't need to multiply 21, 54, and 22. You just need to figure out which fraction in the answer choices has a denominator that $K$ wouldn't be divisible by. How? Well, take a look at (A). In order for $K$ divided by 21 to be an integer, it would have be divisible by 21. It would have to have 21 as a factor. You know 21 is a factor of $K$ because you're told that $K = (21)(54)(22)$. So, you can eliminate (A) because you're looking for the choice that would *not* be an integer. If you look at the rest of the answer choices, you'll notice that none of them mention 21, 54, or 22. Not to worry. If the factors of $K$ include 21, 54, and 22, they must also include the factors of 21, 54, and 22. So, other factors of $K$ include 3 and 7 ($7 \times 3 = 21$), 6 and 9 ($6 \times 9 = 54$), 3 and

18 ($3 \times 18 = 54$), and 2 and 11 ($2 \times 11 = 22$). Any combination of those numbers will form a factor of $K$. Now look at (B). In order for $K$ divided by 27 to be an integer, it would have to have 27 as a factor. Well, look at the list of factors, and you'll see a 9 and a 3, which have a product of 27. That means 27 is a factor of $K$, and is therefore not the answer. Try (C). In order for $K$ divided by 48 to be an integer, it would have to have 48 as a factor. Look at the list of factors. Would any combination of them give you 48? Nope. That means $K$ divided by 48 is *not* an integer, and therefore is the answer. By the way, quickly check out (D) and (E): Can you make 33 with the list of factors? Yes, 11 and 3. Can you make 63? Yes, 9 and 7.

10. **C**     Looks ugly, doesn't it? This is a tough one, but don't worry; you'd never be expected to calculate these. All you need to do is compare. Start by doing a little factoring to change the look of these numbers. In Column A, what's the biggest thing that we can "pull out" of $3^{17}$ and $3^{18}$? You can divide the whole thing, or "pull out" $3^{17}$, so you end up with $3^{17}$ $(1 + 3^1)$, or $3^{17}$ (4). Looks like Column B, doesn't it? The answer is (C).

11. **C**     First of all, figure out what $f$ and $g$ could be. 3 is the remainder when $f$ is divided by 9; if you add the remainder, 3, to the divisor, 9, you'll get a number that works for $f$. $3 + 9 = 12$, so 12 is a value that works for $f$. Check it to make sure: is 3 the remainder when 12 is divided by 9? Yes. 6 is the remainder when $g$ is divided by 9. $6 + 9 = 15$, so 15 is a value that works for $g$. Column B asks for the remainder when $f + g$ is divided by 6. If $f + g$ is $12 + 15$, or 27, what is the remainder when 27 is divided by 6? It's 3. That's the same as Column A, so the answer is (C).

12. **B**     First, there were no variables in this problem, so the answer can't be (D). The word "inclusive" in Column B is the key. "Inclusive" means including 15 and –15 and 0, which must be more than 30 (in Column A). You'll prove it by listing them: –15, –14, –13, –12, –11, –10, –9, –8, –7, –6, –5, –4, –3, –2, –1, 0, 1, 2, 3, 4, 5, 6, 7, 8, 9, 10, 11, 12, 13, 14, 15. That's 31, and that's (B).

**Figures**

1. **A**    In a parallelogram, opposite angles are equal, and the big
           angle plus the small angle adds up to 180 degrees. So
           $x + 120 = 180$. That makes Column A 60, which is bigger
           than the 45 in Column B. The answer is (A).

2. **C**    Draw yourself a picture! To find the area of a slice of the
           pie, first you need to find the area of the whole pie. Then,
           divide the area of the whole pie by 8 to find the area of each
           slice. If the radius of the pie is 6, then the area ($A = \pi r^2$) of
           the whole pie would be $36\pi$. Next, divide $36\pi$ by 8, and you
           get $\frac{9}{2}\pi$. That's (C).

3. **B**    To find the perimeter of triangle $BCD$, first, find the length
           of $BD$ using the Pythagorean theorem. $5^2 + BD^2 = 13^2$.
           Or you may remember that $5^2 + 12^2 = 13^2$. So $BD = 12$. Then,
           you can find the third side of triangle $BCD$. $12^2 + DC^2 = 15^2$.
           Notice that this is a 3:4:5 right triangle. So $DC$ is 9. Next,
           add up the sides of triangle $BCD$. $9 + 12 + 15 = 36$. So,
           Column A is 36. Because Column B is 42, (B) is the answer.

4. **A**    A line has 180 degrees, so $a + 20 + b = 180$. That means
           that $a + b = 160$. You're also told that $a = 3b$. So, plug in
           those answer choices for $b$: (C) $b = 25$, so $a = 75$. Does
           $25 + 75 = 160$? Nope, it's 100, too small. (B) $b = 30$, so
           $a = 90$. Does $30 + 90 = 160$? Nope, it's 120, too small. Bet
           the answer's (A). Double-check to make sure. (A) $b = 40$, so
           $a = 120$. Does $40 + 120 = 160$? Yes. That's the answer.

5. **C**    To find the value of $n$, start with the right triangle for which
           you're given two of the three sides. Use the Pythagorean
           theorem: $15^2 + b^2 = 25^2$. Notice that this is a 3:4:5 right trian-
           gle; $15 = 3(5)$ and $25 = 5(5)$. So $b = 20$ or $4(5)$. Now you have
           two of the three sides of the triangle: $12^2 + n^2 = 20$. Notice
           that you've got another 3:4:5 right triangle. $12 = 3(4)$ and
           $20 = 5(4)$. So $n = 4(4)$ or 16. That's (C).

6. **E**    Draw yourself a picture! To find the perimeter of a
           rectangle, you need to know the length and the width. If
           the newspaper ad with a width of 14 has the same area as
           another ad 52 long and 28 wide, that means that

14 (length) = 52(28). Divide both sides by 14, and you get length = 52(2) = 104. So, the dimensions of our mystery ad are 104 + 104 + 14 + 14. Add them up and you get 236. That's (E).

7. **C**   Triangle $ABC$ is isosceles. That means that the base and the height are each equal to 4. So the base of the unshaded region is 3, because the base of the shaded region is 1. The area of triangle $ABC$ is $\frac{1}{2}(4)(4)$, or 8. The area of triangle $ABD$ is $\frac{1}{2}(4)(3)$, or 6. Subtract the area of $ABD$ from the area of $ABC$ to get the area of the shaded region, $BCD$. That's 8 – 6, which is 2. So, in Column A, the area of the shaded region, 2, divided by the area of the unshaded region, 6, is $\frac{2}{6}$, or $\frac{1}{3}$. The answer is (C).

8. **B**   To find the perimeter of the figure, you need to add up all the sides. To find the missing side of the rectangle, solve for the opposite side of the rectangle, using the Pythagorean theorem: $a^2 + b^2 = c^2$. You may remember that $5^2 + 12^2 = 13^2$. So the missing sides of the rectangle are each 13. Now, add up the sides of the figure: 5 + 12 + 17 + 13 + 17 = 64. That's (B).

9. **B**   Draw yourself a picture! The formula for circumference is $C = \pi d$, also known as $2\pi r$. Because $r = \frac{1}{2}$, $C = (2)\pi \left(\frac{1}{2}\right)$, or $\pi$. So you have $\pi$ in Column A and 4 in Column B. Remember that $\pi$ is equal to a little more than 3. That means the answer is (B).

10. **A**   Draw yourself a picture! Plug in some numbers and see what happens. To start with, make $r = 2$. Then, you get $2\pi r = 4\pi$ (which is about 12-ish) in Column A and 4(2) = 8 in Column B. So Column A is greater if $r = 2$. Eliminate choices (B) and (C). Now plug in a weird number;

make $r = \frac{1}{2}$. Then you get $\pi$ in Column A and 2 in Column B. Column A wins again. You can't plug in 0 or a negative number because $r$ is the radius of the circle and the side of the square. The answer is (A).

11. **D**  Remember, if you don't get a diagram, draw one yourself. Your little map should form a 3:4:5 right triangle, so the street from the supermarket to the beauty parlor is 5 blocks long. Drawing your own diagram makes this problem so much easier!

12. **D**  Because the question mentions $\pi$, but the answer choices don't, start by rounding off $\pi$ to 3, so the gear travels 9 inches per revolution ($3\pi = 9$, roughly). After all, the question says "approximately," so approximate! The gear makes 12 revolutions per minute, so that's 12 revs times 9 inches, which is 108 inches per minute. The question asks about feet per hour, so first, convert minutes to hours, by multiplying 108 times 60 (because there are 60 minutes in an hour), and we get 6,480 inches per hour. Now, convert inches to feet by dividing that by 12 (there are 12 inches in a foot) and you get 540. Now, which answer choice is closest to 540? That would be (D).

## Equations I

1. **C**  In Column A, $\frac{30}{100}$ (150) = $\frac{30}{10}$ (150) = 3(15) = 45. In Column B, $\frac{60}{100}$ (75) = $\frac{3}{5}$ (75) = 3(15) = 45. The answer is (C).

2. **B**  Remember the formula: Average = $\dfrac{\text{Total}}{\text{Number}}$. In this case, you have the average, 17, and the number, 2. That makes the total 34. In other words, the two numbers have to add up to 34, but neither of them can be 12 or less. Because Column A is asking for twice the larger of the two integers, figure out what the largest integer could be by pairing it with the smallest integer we can use, or 13. If the total is

34, and one number is 13, that means the other number is 21 because 21 + 13 = 34. So, in Column A, we get 42, which is twice 21. We have 44 in Column B, so (B) is the answer.

3. **D** First of all, do a little ballparking. If a one-hour call costs $7.20, a ten-minute call must cost much less. Eliminate (A). Now, make a proportion, but first, change "one hour" into "60 minutes," because you're comparing it to ten minutes. So, you have: $\frac{\text{cost}}{\text{minutes}} = \frac{7.20}{60} = \frac{x}{10}$. A little cross-multiplying gets you $60x = (7.20)(10)$, or $60x = 72$. Divide both sides by 60 and you get $x = 1.20$. That's (D).

4. **C** Remember the formula: Average = $\frac{\text{Total}}{\text{Number}}$. In Column A, the average is 7 + 3 + 4 + 2, or 16, divided by 4, which is 4. In Column B, you have to find the average of $2a + 5$, $4a$, and $7 - 6a$. Why not plug in something for $a$ to make this easier? How about 2? Now you're finding the average of 9, 8, and –5. 9 + 8 – 5 = 12, divided by the number of numbers, which is 3, gives 4. So far the answer is (C). Plug in again—something weird this time, just to be sure. How about 0? Now you're finding the average of 5, 0, and 7. 12 divided by the number of numbers, which is 3, gives 4. Again, you get (C). By the way, you could also have solved Column B by adding everything up as is: $2a + 5 + 4a + 7 - 6a = 12$. 12 divided by the number of numbers, which is 3, gives 4.

5. **C** It's tempting to think that the two discounts add up to 55 percent. But it just isn't true. Test it out by plugging in the perfect percent number: 100. A 30 percent discount from $100 is $30. If that's followed by a 25 percent, that would be

a $25 discount of the 70 remaining dollars. So, 25 percent, or one-fourth, of 70 is $17.50. So $p$, or the two discounts together, are $30 + $17.50, or $47.50. That's the number in Column B, isn't it? So, the answer is (C).

6. **C** Remember those quadratic equations? Doesn't $m^2 + 2mn + n^2$ look exactly like $x^2 + 2xy + y^2$, which equals $(x + y)^2$? That means you could rewrite $m^2 + 2mn + n^2$ as $(m + n)^2$. Now, you're also told that $m + n = p$, which means that $p$ and $m + n$ are interchangeable. If you replace the $m + n$ in the $(m + n)^2$ with the $p$, you get $p^2$. So, $m^2 + 2mn + n^2 = (m + n)^2 = p^2$. That's (C). Whew! But hey—you can also plug in on this one: 2 for $m$, 3 for $n$, and 5 for $p$—we get $2^2 + (2)(2)(3) + 3^2$, which equals 25. That's our target answer. Now, to the answers.

   (A)   $(4)(5) = 20$. Eliminate.
   (B)   $15 - 2 = 13$. Eliminate.
   (C)   $(5)^2 = 25$. Bingo!
   (D)   $(5)^2 + 4(2 + 5) = 25 + 28 = 53$. Eliminate.
   (E)   $(5)^2 + (3)(5) + (2)^2 = 25 + 15 + 4 = 44$. Eliminate.

It's (C)!

7. **E** Don't worry, there's no such thing as a "∗." This is one of those funny-symboled function problems. This time, you don't have numbers to use. Sounds like a plug in! Plug in $x = 3$ and $y = 2$. First, you'll do the $x \approx y$ in the parentheses. You know that $x * y = x(x - y)$, so $3(3 - 2) = 3(1) = 3$. So, $x * (x * y)$ can be rewritten as $x * 3$. Now, remembering that you made $x = 3$, the question really is $3 * 3 = 3(3 - 3) = 3(0) = 0$. That's the target you're looking for in the answer choices: 0. So, plug in $x = 3$ and $y = 2$ in the answer choices, and look for 0.

   (A)  Does $x^2 - xy = 0$? $(3)^2 - (3)(2) = 9 - 6 = 3$. Nope.
   (B)  Does $x^2 - 2xy = 0$? $(3)^2 - 2(3)(2) = 9 - 12 = -3$. Nope.
   (C)  Does $x^3 - x^2 - xy = 0$? $(3)^3 - (3)^2 - (3)(2) = 27 - 9 - 6 = 12$. Nope.
   (D)  Does $x^3 - (xy)^2 = 0$? $(3)^3 - \{(3)(2)\}^2 = 27 - 36 = -9$. Nope.
   (E)  Does $x^2 - x^3 + x^2y = 0$? $(3)^2 - (3)^3 + \{(3)^2(2)\} = 9 - 27 + 18 = 0$. Bingo!

8. **C**    Go to the graph and find January 1971 to April 1978. Use Process of Elimination. The greatest amount of private donations to charitable causes for that period was to the category of Child Safety. Eliminate (D). The second greatest was Other. Eliminate choice (E). The third greatest was Environmental Protection. That's (C).

9. **D**    This question requires you to find the amount of money received by Child Safety organizations in September 1989 from the left-hand chart. It was $9.4 million. Then, divide that amount by the number of Child Safety organizations—38 (from the right-hand chart). It's time to ballpark! To make it as easy as possible, round both of those figures up. Pretend it's $10 million divided by 40. That's $250,000. That's (D).

10. **C**   Go to the graph and find September 1985 to December 1989. The amount donated to Homeless Aid causes for that period was about $300 million. The amount donated to Animal Rights causes for that period was about $225 million. You can reduce ratios! The ratio of 300:225 reduces to 12:9, or 4:3. That's (C).

11. **A**   First of all, there are only numbers in this problem, so the answer cannot be (D). Now, the formula for percent increase is the difference divided by the original, multiplied by 100. In Column A, the difference (between 4 and 5) is 1, and the original number is 4, so that's $\frac{1}{4}$. Multiply that by 100 and you get 25%. In Column B, the difference (between 4 and 5) is 1, but the original number is 5, so that's $\frac{1}{5}$. Multiply that by 100 and you get 20%. 25% is bigger than 20%, so the answer is (A).

12. **A**   First, there are no variables in the problem, so the answer can't be (D). Now, because Column B is already in percent form, convert Column A also to a percent. It will be easier

to compare the two columns. 0.01 is the same as $\frac{1}{100}$ which is the same as 1%. Well, 1% is bigger than $\frac{1}{8}$%, so the answer is (A).

## Equations II

1. **E**   Plug in a number for $a$. How about 10? So, Alex gave Jonathan 10 dollars. She gave Gina two dollars more than she gave Jonathan, so she gave Gina 12 dollars. She gave Louanne three dollars less than she gave Gina, so she gave Louanne 9 dollars. So altogether, Alex gave Gina, Jonathan, and Louanne 10 + 12 + 9, or 31 dollars. (By the way, just ignore that "in terms of $a$." Because you plugged in, you're not answering the question in terms of $a$ anymore.) Now check the answers, plugging in 10 for $a$, and looking for the target answer, 31.

    (A)  Does $\frac{10}{3}$ = 31? Nope.

    (B)  Does 10 − 1 = 31? Nope.

    (C)  Does 3(10) = 31? Nope.

    (D)  Does 3(10) − 1 = 31? Nope.

    (E)  Does 3(10) + 1 = 31? Yes. The answer is (E).

2. **D**   You're being told that $3x = -2$, so plug in −2 for $3x$ in $(3x - 3)2$. This gives you $(-2 - 3)2 = (-5)2 = 25$. That's (D).

3. **D**   Which costs more, the car or the paint job? The car. What do the answer choices represent? The cost of the car. Ballpark first. If the combined cost was $4,800, and the biggest chunk of that is the cost of the car, choices (A) and (B), are ridiculously low. A $4,000 paint job for an $800 car? No way. Eliminate those choices. What choices are left? (C), (D), and (E). Start plugging in the middle of those values, (D), $4,000. Hey, it's also the easiest number to work with, so why not? You're told that the cost of the paint job was $\frac{1}{5}$ the cost of the car. One-fifth of $4,000 is $800 (now you see where that trap answer choice came from). Is $4,000 plus $800 equal to $4,800? Yes. You're done—the answer is (D).

4. **E**  Start with $x = y$. Plug in 4 for both $x$ and $y$. Now, put that into the first equation to get $z$; $4 + 4 = 8$, so $z = 8$. Next, go to the answers, plugging in 4 for $x$ and $y$ and 8 for $z$.

(A)  $2(4) + 2(4) = 2(8)$. $8 + 8 = 16$. That's true.

(B)  $4 - 4 = 0$. That's true.

(C)  $4 - 8 = 4 - 8$. That's true.

(D)  $4 = \frac{8}{2}$. That's true.

(E)  $4 - 4 = 2(8)$. $0 = 16$? That's not true, and because this is an EXCEPT question, (E) is the answer.

5. **A**  Plug in 2 for $x$ and 3 for $y$—that makes $xy$ an even integer.

(A)  $(2)(3) + 5 = 11$. That's odd, so leave it in.

(B)  $2 + 3 = 5$. That's odd, so leave it in.

(C)  $\frac{2}{3}$. That's not an integer, so eliminate it.

(D)  $4(2) = 8$. That's even, so eliminate it.

(E)  $7(2)(3) = 42$. That's even, so eliminate it.

So, you got rid of choices (C), (D), and (E). But standard operating procedure on a "must be" question says we need to plug in twice; otherwise, how would we choose between (A) and (B)? At first, you made $x$ even and $y$ odd. Make them both even and just change $y$ to 4. Is $xy$ even, using these numbers? Yes, it's 8. Go back to the two remaining choices.

(A)  $(2)(3) + 5 = 13$. That's still odd, so leave it in.
(B)  $2 + 4 = 6$. That's even, so eliminate it. The answer is (A).

6. **C**  Use those answer choices! Because the question is asking for the least number, start by plugging in (A), the least number in the answer choices.

(A)  Does $\{3(-3) + 2\} \{-3 - 3\} = 0$? $(-7)(-6) = -42$, which isn't 0.

(B)  Does $\{3(-2) + 2\} \{-2 - 2\} = 0$? $(-4)(-4) = -16$, which isn't 0.

(C)  Does $\{3(-\frac{2}{3}) + 2\} \{-\frac{2}{3} - 3\} = 0$? $(0)(-3\frac{2}{3}) = 0$. Bingo!

7. **D**    First, plug in an easy number. How about $x = 2$? That gives us 3 as the quantity in Column A and $-1$ as the quantity in Column B. We know that 3 is greater than $-1$; *so far* the answer is (A). Eliminate (B) and (C) on your scratch paper. For our second round of plugging in, try $x = 0$. That gives us 1 in Column A and 1 in Column B—now the two columns are equal. You plugged in *different* numbers, you got *different* answers. Therefore, the answer is (D).

8. **B**    The information about tips is the catch. Its only purpose is to cause careless errors. Confront this trap by reducing the day's total by $20—to $160. What we're left with is a very straightforward problem. If each customer bought 2 four-dollar dishes, then each customer spent $8 on food. Now you can plug in the answer choices:
(A) Does 18 equal 160 divided by 8? Nope.
(B) Does 20 equal 160 divided by 8? Yes.
(C) Does 22 equal 160 divided by 8? Nope.
(D) Does 40 equal 160 divided by 8? Nope.
(E) Does 44 equal 160 divided by 8? Nope.

By the way, you also could have divided $160 by $8 to get 20. The answer is (B).

9. **C**    Don't forget to plug in on geometry problems with variables. Plugging In according to the rule of 180, You can make $a = 50$, and make the other two angles inside the triangle 60 and 70. Because $b$ and $c$ are vertical to the other angles in the triangle, $b + c = 130$ in Column A. $180 - 50 = 130$ in Column B. The answer is (C).

10. **C**    With all of these percents, wouldn't it be nice to have a total number? Just plug one in. Make the total number of voters 100 (the best number to plug in when you're dealing with percents). 60 percent of the voters are women, so that's 60 women, and the remaining voters are men, so that's 40 (we made the total 100, remember?) men. 30 percent of the women would be 30 percent of 60, which is $\frac{30}{100}$ (60), or 18 women, who voted for candidate X. 20 per-

cent of the men would be 20 percent of 40, which is $\frac{20}{100}$ (40), or 8 men, who voted for candidate X. So, the total number of people voting for candidate X is 18 + 8, or 26. Because your total is 100, 26 is equal to 26 percent. That's (C).

11. **D**   First, plug in a pair of easy numbers. Try 3 for $x$ and 4 for $y$. (4 is a good plug-in for $y$, because $\sqrt{4}$ is an integer.) This gives 12 for Column A and 6 for Column B. With these plug-ins, choice (A) works, which means you can eliminate choices (B) and (C). But you have to plug in again, because you still have choice (D) to contend with. Plug in some weird numbers. How about 0 for $x$ and 0 for $y$? (There's no rule that says $x$ and $y$ have to be different.) That gives 0 for Column A and 0 for Column B. Because these numbers make the two columns equal, this proves that A is not always the answer, and the correct answer is (D).

12. **B**   Plug in those answer choices! There are two conditions on the answer. First, its second digit must be 3 times the first digit. Because ETS's answer must satisfy both conditions, you can eliminate any choice that fails to satisfy either of them. Therefore, you tackle one condition at a time. Choice (C): Is 6 three times 3? No. Eliminate. Choice (B): Is 6 three times 2? Yes. A possibility. Choice (D): Is 2 three times 6? No. Eliminate. Choice (A): Is 3 three times 1? Yes. A possibility. Choice (E): Is 3 three times 9? No. Eliminate. You've already narrowed it down to two possibilities, choices (A) and (B). Now you apply the second condition, that the reversed form of the number must be 36 more than the original number. Check the remaining choices: Choice (A): Is 31 equal to 36 more than 13? No. Eliminate. That's it, the answer must be (B). Check it to make sure: 62 *is* exactly 36 more than 26.

# Don't Stop Now...

## Get More

**More Test Prep**—If you're looking to learn more about how to raise your GRE score, you're in the right place. We offer private tutoring, small group tutoring, classroom courses, online courses, and an array of books.

**More Books**—If you like *Crash Course for GRE*, you might want to check out some of our other titles:

*Word Smart for the GRE*

*Verbal Workout for the GRE*

*Cracking the GRE*

*Cracking the GRE with DVD*

*Graduate School Companion*

**More Acceptance Letters**—We know more than just tests. We know a lot about graduate school admissions, too. We've got tips for crafting the perfect essay and much more.

To learn more about any of our private tutoring programs, small group tutoring, classroom courses, or online courses, please call **800-2Review** (800-273-8439) or visit **PrincetonReview.com/GRE.**

The Princeton Review